T0315673

DERBYSHIRE'S HIGH PEAK

AIR CRASH SITES

SOUTHERN REGION

Books by the Author

Non-fiction
Bomb on the Red Markers
Fighter! Fighter! Corkscrew Port!
The Fear In the Sky
Through Enemy Skies
We Kept 'Em Flying

Peakland Air Crashes Series:
The South (2005)
The Central Area (2006)
The North (2006)

Derbyshire's High Peak Air Crash Sites, Northern Region
High Peak Air Crash Sites, Central Region
Derbyshire's High Peak Air Crash Sites, Southern Region
White Peak Air Crash Sites

Faction
A Magnificent Diversion Series
(Acclaimed by the First World War Aviation Historical Society)
The Infinite Reaches 1915–16
Contact Patrol 1916
Sold A Pup 1917
The Great Disservice 1918

Blind Faith: Joan Waste, Derby's Martyr
Joyce Lewis of Mancetter, Lichfield's Feisty Martyr

Fiction
In Kinder's Mists (a Kinderscout ghost story)
Though the Treason Pleases (Irish Troubles)

DERBYSHIRE'S HIGH PEAK
AIR CRASH SITES
SOUTHERN REGION

Pat Cunningham, DFM

'With map-reading skills like yours you need a GPS'

Wiesława White

Front cover image: Volunteer Ranger Neil Broadbent and Ashley Steadman, formerly of Headquarters, National Air Traffic Service, with Dylan (left) and Bella (right), on Shining Tor

First published 2014 by DB Publishing, an imprint of JMD Media Ltd, Nottingham, United Kingdom.

Copyright © Pat Cunningham 2014

All Rights Reserved. No part of this publication may be reproduced, stored in a retrieval system, or transmitted in any form, or by any means, electronic, mechanical, photocopying, recording or otherwise without the prior permission in writing of the copyright holders, nor be otherwise circulated in any form or binding or cover other than in which it is published and without a similar condition being imposed on the subsequent publisher.

ISBN 9781780913742

Printed and bound by Copytech (UK) Limited, Peterborough.

Contents

Private publications by the Author

'*Now We Are Ninety*' (tribute to mother ...)

'*The Elephant Box, Volumes 1 # 2*' (a grandfather's tall tales)

'*By Fell and Dale, Volumes 1 # 5*' (walker's logs)

'*Frozen Tears*' (a Polish family's wartime odyssey)

'*Flotsam*' (short pieces)

'*Jetsam*' (short pieces)

Autobiographical Series:

'*Brat to Well Beloved*' (RAF Aircraft Apprentice to Air Electronics Officer)

[And, vice Gilbert and Sullivan ...]

'*Apprentice to a Pilot*' (RAF pilot training)

'*The Kind Commander*' (RAF captaincy)

'*The Simple Captain*' (civil captaincy)

In preparation:

'*Frozen Tears*' (wartime romance)

'*The Ignorant Walker's Companion*' (a walker's reflections)

'*The Tenant*'/'*The CEO*' (experiences of a housing association)

'*Fifty Years Of Peace: 1945-1995*' [Celebratory Stones in Derbyshire] (Memoirs of RAF 'peacekeeping' personnel from Malaya to the First Gulf War)

Pat Cunningham,
DFM, BA, Lic Ac, cfs, RAF, 2014

INTRODUCTION

The air crashes in this book occurred between Edale, in Derbyshire's High Peak, and Wildboarclough, to the south of Buxton, on the fringes of the White Peak. The northerly sites, therefore, are on upper moorland, while the southerly ones, though never far from high ground, tend to be in more accessible terrain.

This means that debris from the southern sites was more easily disposed of, the land being returned to production the moment it was cleared; just as happened on the farmlands of Waterloo, and indeed, of the Somme, although clearing the latter took a while longer. Yet there are some who regard the higher-altitude air-crash sites as shrines simply by virtue of their uncleared debris. But debris can only be transitory, and if officially-sponsored markers were provided then the walker-driven distinction observed in this series between sites with and without surface debris would become irrelevant.

As it is, where no debris is left, a metal detector almost invariably provides evidence. In some cases a shallow crater might remain, or some interested group might have erected a memorial – not always appropriate, and oft-times inaccurate –, but little else. Never forgetting that the majority of site visits draw the walker into magnificent scenery.

Only not quite all, for the geographical focus of this series is northern Mercia, and in running from Lichfield to Huddersfield, it touches urban Manchester and totally embraces Sheffield.

That said, none of the sites is more than fifteen minutes from a recognised path; nor is this area's crash-site seeker faced with unremitting moorland. Indeed, once south of Edale's Rufforth Edge the terrain becomes decidedly less remote. Yet the airy Shining Tor ridge, the summit of Axe Edge, and the soaring rise of Shutlingsloe, all challenge. All too, require the walker to anticipate worsening weather, at the very least by wearing sensible clothing and packing food and drink. They also call for a map and compass to be carried; backed, of course, by a working knowledge of how to use them. And while not essential, a GPS is very comforting; ideally one with a map! Not forgetting spare batteries.

The walkers' guides following each narrative are routes the author has taken, while the crash-site co-ordinates have been checked on numerous occasions. The GPS-derived elevations, though, are only a rough indicator, as are any timings.

As for the tragedies themselves, almost all occurred because airmen made a mistake. Most commonly through ignoring the flight-safety doggerel advising, 'And if you'd end up safe and sound, Don't fly through cloud to find the ground'.

Of course, descending blind was common practice, fliers did it all the time, and for the most part got away with it, emerging into the clear and seeing their airfield, if not quite where they had expected it to be, not more than a mere nudge of the stick off ... Those who came to grief in this district, however, were invariably convinced that they were approaching the low-lying coastal airfield for which their altimeter had been set, not knowing that they had drifted off course and with no notion, therefore, that the healthily-seeming altitude now indicated on its dial was filled with solid gritstone.

To the aviator-walker, accordingly, with fingers humbly crossed, the true interest in such tragic sites lies in the flight-safety lessons they taught others. But off-path walking has lessons to teach too. Chief among them, not to hurry, and to constantly watch for concealed boulders and peat holes. Also, breathtaking though the scenery may be, to stop before gazing around to take it in!

THE AIR-CRASH DEBRIS

The co-ordinates given reflect, in the main, where debris has been pooled. But when an aircraft impacted at descent speed the scatter was often widespread. Then again, because surface debris might deflect a future air search, the salvage teams would bury or burn what they could not remove. Much of what is seen today, therefore, was excavated by early enthusiasts or exposed by subsequent movement of the peat.

It is reluctantly accepted that for many walkers surface debris defines a site. Yet the stories behind each tragedy lose nothing for a lack of visible metal. To reiterate, virtually all the sites have been verified by metal-detecting, with a very few being determined by contemporary photographs and by verifiable witness reports. But having reached the site, and after due reflection, do spare time for the scenery!

Pat Cunningham, DFM, 2014 (RAF 1951–1973)

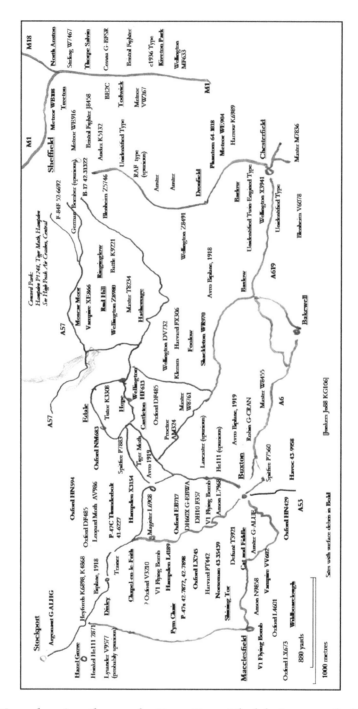

Area Map, showing the crash sites, *sites with debris are emboldened*

These are crash sites where debris remained on the surface in 2014; in a few cases where a memorial has been erected, or a discernible crater exists.

Edale

1. Airspeed Oxford Mk.1 HN594
Brown Knoll, Edale

SK 08189 85204 558 m
Unit and Station: No. 21 (Pilots) Advanced Flying Unit, RAF Seighford (north-west of Stafford), No. 21 Group, Flying Training Command
Date: 28 December 1945
Crew: three, all injured:
- Warrant Officer George Robinson, pilot, pilot-navigation instructor
- Flying Officer John E. Dowthwaite, pilot on course
- Flying Officer Edward A. Croker, pilot on course

On 28 December 1945 Flying Officer John Dowthwaite and Flying Officer Edward Croker were detailed to fly a daytime pilot-navigation exercise under the tutelage of staff instructor Warrant Officer George Robinson. Having just returned from flying duties in South Africa the two were being re-introduced, among other things, to flying in UK weather conditions. Fifty minutes into the flight, therefore, with just 1,000 feet showing on the altimeter when cloud closed in to blot out the snow-fringed terrain below, both of them expressed concern about the proximity of the 2,088-foot spot height of Kinder Scout shown on the chart. Warrant Officer Robinson merely laughed, assuring them that he knew the area like the back of his hand. Even so he initiated a climb. Moments later, however, the aircraft struck the ground, bounced, then hit hard, disintegrating and throwing the unharnessed Flying Officer Croker clear.

Providentially there was no fire, for when Flying Officer Croker hobbled back on what he believed to be broken ankles – in fact, they were very severely sprained –, he found his fellow aircrew badly injured amidst the wreckage.

Press photo of the crash

In view of the poor visibility, and aware that their Seighford base had no record of the proposed route, there seemed little chance of them being found in the near future. With that in mind, and having wrapped both casualties in parachutes for warmth, Flying Officer Croker set off to seek assistance.

What followed was an epic, for the crash had occurred just below the summit of Brown Knoll. Whether Flying Officer Croker used the topographical map, or made his way by chance, he headed towards the Vale, and the nearest succour. Even so, forced to crawl for much of the time, he had to cover a tortuous two miles until he came to Upper Booth where a lady, having tended to his immediate needs, walked on to Edale, and the nearest telephone, to raise the alarm.

A search was instituted, but conditions were so poor that, after nine hours, it was called off. Indeed, not until mid-morning next day did an aircraft locate the crash.

The two injured airmen, clad as they were only in battledress and despite the parachute covering, were lucky to survive. As it was, Warrant Officer Robinson had to have a leg amputated.

For his part, Flying Officer Croker went on to play football for Charlton and to become secretary of the Football Association. As for former-Warrant Officer Robinson, despite his disability he took to making his way to the site on the anniversary of the crash. In fact, on the fortieth anniversary all three men foregathered, when, as Peak Park Ranger Peter Jackson recalled, John Dowthwaite told him feelingly, 'You can't imagine the gratitude I felt as George and I lay there in the wreckage, knowing that, despite his pain, Ted Croker had gone off to do his best for us.'

Ted and Mary Dalton, then farming at Kinder Farm, Chapel-en-le-Frith, visited the crash just days later. Mrs Dalton smiled. 'We rolled one of the plane's wheels back with us.' Her husband grunted. 'I'd thought of using it in a wheelbarrow, but it was too big. Though we used one of the seats as a children's swing for years afterwards.' The major part of the wreckage, they remembered, was recovered via the remote Shireoaks Farm.

The trio, reunited

VISITING THE SITE

From the Edale direction the most convenient public parking is in the large lay-by, marked on the map, at SK 10797 84713 (250 m), just past Barber Booth. Although the metalled road continues beyond Upper Booth it is then gated to private vehicles. The path – a section of the Pennine Way – ascends Jacob's Ladder, either by the steps or by the zig-zag, to SK 08077 86113 (533 m). Here, somewhat short of Edale Cross, the Brown Knoll path leads off, initially south-eastwards. The site lies 200 yards short of the Knoll at SK 08258 85267 (560 m), 100 yards off-path to the right. In early 2013 there was a moderate amount of wreckage, but situated amid hags and groughs.

The debris pool, 2013

2. Republic P-47C Thunderbolt 41-6227
Horsehill Tor, Hope Valley

SK 09344 84337 492 m

Unit and Station: United States Eighth Army Air Force,
56th Fighter Group, 63rd Fighter Squadron,
AAF123 (RAF Horsham St Faith), Norwich

Date: 25 April 1943

Crew: pilot, baled out, fractured spine

* Second Lieutenant John E. Coenen, USAAF

On 25 April 1943, Easter Sunday, Second Lieutenant John Coenen had not long left Liverpool's Speke airfield on his return from a stores run when he found that weather conditions over the Peakland hills had deteriorated markedly. He was reasonably experienced, with just under 500 hours' flying time and almost 260 hours on Thunderbolts, but as a day-fighter pilot he would have been most accustomed to clear-sky operations. Well aware that the P-47 Thunderbolt's prized nippiness in roll did not make it a good platform for rough-air flying on instruments, he decided to turn back. He reported later that, as he did so, rough currents in the thick cloud had virtually rolled him over, that his controls had grown sluggish, and that as the machine began to turn rapidly he had concluded that he was in a spin.

Shocked by the suddenness of this loss of control, only too well aware of the high ground nearby, and realising that he was of far more value than the aeroplane, Second Lieutenant Coenen tried to abandon. Only to have flight forces hold him into his seat. Just as well, then, that he had not delayed, for such forces suggest that, rather than a spin, the aircraft was in an increasing-speed spiral dive, a flight condition which required a significantly different recovery technique from that of a spin.

It was his too-hastily streamed parachute that finally extracted him from the cockpit, but it then snagged the tailplane, providentially tearing free again seconds later.

'I came down very fast,' he wrote later, 'hitting hard, hurting my back, and coming to rest on my stomach.'

As it happened, his speedy descent had been seen by hikers near Lee Farm. These stalwarts, appreciating that he had suffered a back injury, commandeered a farm gate for use as a stretcher and carried him back to the farm. After which one of them trekked to the nearest phone, at Edale, to summon help.

Lee Farm

Mr Alan Chapman, of Barber Booth, also saw the parachute emerge from the clouds. 'It was a Sunday,' he recalled, 'and we were going to the Methodist Chapel when we heard this aeroplane coming hell for leather. Then its engine stopped. And moments later we saw the parachute coming down.'

As Mr Roy Cooper, of Highfield Farm, Upper Booth, remembered, 'The plane dived straight out of the clouds into our Cartledge field: I remember the plume of smoke coming up. Then the parachute appeared. As for the pilot, he was shocked, and in pain, but all he seemed to be worried about was that the crash might stop him flying.'

It did not. Indeed, five months later, on 27 September 1943, Second Lieutenant Coenen got airborne on his thirteenth operational mission, a deep-penetration escort sortie to Emden, notwithstanding that he had begun suffering severe discomfort whenever pulling tight turns: the basic stock-in-trade of any fighter pilot. On the return leg, however, his inability to manoeuvre to full effect left him out of position at a moment when a bomber element particularly required his protection. Seeing the gap, the opportunist Focke-Wulf 190s streamed in. But, fortunately for Second Lieutenant Coenen's future peace of mind, the ensuing melee allowed him to down one of them. On top of which, in rejoining the now-scattered escorts, he shot down a second as it was in the very act of stalking one of his fellow Thunderbolt pilots, so forestalling any conceivable charge that in concealing his back pain he had endangered either his charges or his section.

But that was it, for a post-landing medical examination finally revealed that, in baling out all those months before, he had sustained two spinal fractures; in view of which, no longer fit to fly, he was returned to the United States. But with the solace of holding the Air Medal, and the two bronze oak leaf clusters denoting a triple award of that worthy decoration.

The accident investigation into the Edale crash had found the violent weather entirely to blame. Just the same, it had recommended that Second Lieutenant Coenen would have been better served had he obtained a written flight-forecast rather than the 'conversational' met update he had received at Speke; although quite how that would have helped is difficult to see, when Second Lieutenant Coenen had so recently transited the area on his outbound leg.

As for the abandoned P-47, on plunging into a moorland shoulder far above the Lee Farm path, on the southern slope of Horsehill Tor, it was found to have impacted at high speed: a spiral dive then, and not a slow-speed spin.

VISITING THE SITE

The closest public parking is in the generous lay-by at SK 10797 84713 (250 m), just past Barber Booth. From here the simplest way to the site leads along the Pennine Way and up Jacob's Ladder to the Brown Knoll path. It then passes the Knoll and continues for 0.6 miles, to SK 09045 85459 (530 m) before entering a south-westerly running gully. 300 yards down the gully is the substantial Dalehead Cairn, the impact site lying 100 yards to the left, on 060°M. In late 2013 a moderate pool of debris remained. In poor weather the descent may be made, with due care, following the gully down to Dalehead.

The debris pool looking towards the Dalehead Cairn

3. Handley Page Hampden Mk.1 X3154
Rushup Edge

SK 10418 82999 511 m
Unit and Station: No. 106 Squadron, RAF Finningley (near Doncaster),
No. 5 Group, Bomber Command
Date: 21 December 1940
Crew: four, all killed
• Pilot Officer Michael Hubbard, pilot
• Sergeant Kenneth Walsingham Boyd Perkins, pilot, acting as
  navigator
• Sergeant Derrick Joseph Davey, wireless operator/air gunner
• Sergeant David William Smith, wireless operator/air gunner

In late 1940 No. 106 Squadron's main operational task was to lay mines in harbours where the Germans were readying invasion barges. It combined this with converting crews to the Hampden, a function undertaken later by specialist 'Operational Training Units'.

When Pilot Officer Michael Hubbard took off with his trainee crew in Hampden X3154 on 21 December 1940, he had flown just twenty-three hours on the type out of a moderate 310 hours' total flying. It is not known, however, what experience Sergeant Kenneth Perkins, a fellow pilot, had in the role of navigator. What is known is that they crashed fifty miles off their intended track.

The night navigational exercise from RAF Finningley had sent them into the Midlands area, but on a route designed to avoid its high ground. Yet even though it was a clear night the aircraft was seen to approach from the Eldon Hill Quarry area to the south, and to fly without deviating into Rushup Edge, striking and bursting into flames at 1,700 feet above sea level.

The official inquiry would castigate both pilot and navigator on three counts: for being lost so far off track, and therefore over high ground, without realising it; for flying so low; and for their failure to utilise their W/T set (wireless-telegraphy: morse) to aid their navigation.

Although the crew were clearly oblivious to the danger as they app-roached Rushup Edge, some would-be rescuers initially deduced that one crew member had attempted to jump before impact, his body having been found some way short of the crash site. This was later attributed, however, the extreme steepness of the slope. Indeed, Mr Billy Dakin, who farmed the area, remembered that when a rope broke during the salvage operation a heavy engine, likewise, careered all the way down to the road, hazarding the support vehicles parked there.

Researcher Professor Sean Moran, at the debris pool, looking towards Rushup Edge Farm

Heat exploded 0303 inch calibre cartridge embedded in molten debris

Simple (isothermal) Altimeter dial, from the Rushup Hampden,
courtesy Frank Worsley

VISITING THE SITE

Adequate parking is available at Mam Tor. The track to the site leads westwards from the Barber Booth road at SK 12497 83429 (457 m), or rather more easily, at SK12475 83385 (432 m). Whichever is chosen, having followed the Rushup Edge track for 1.34 miles, to SK 10379 83062 (515 m), the site is 100 yards downslope to the left. An alternative path runs south of the boundary wall and leads through a series of farm gates each of which, until recent replacements were installed, featured novel latches.

In early 2013 just a few chunks of molten metal remained, and even then the heat-exploded 0.303-inch calibre cartridge in one had been levered out …

4. Airspeed Oxford Mk.1 NM683
Rushup Edge, lower northern slopes

SK 10944 83827 270m

Unit and Station: Navigation Training Unit, Pathfinder Force, RAF Warboys (near Huntingdon), No. 8 Group, Bomber Command

Date 4 March 1945

Crew: four, all injured

* Flight Lieutenant Brian Gipson, DFC and bar, pilot
* Flight Lieutenant Barclay, DFC, navigator, staff instructor
* Flying Officer Skone-Reese, DFC, bomb aimer
* Flight Lieutenant D.I. Jones, passengering pilot

Oxford cockpit

In March 1945, when a pilot was to be transported to Royal Naval Air Station Stretton, near Warrington, the Navigational Training Unit of Bomber Command's Pathfinder Force met the requirement by laying on a map-reading cross-country exercise.

To a man, the occupants of Oxford NM683, were experienced operationally, as their decorations bear witness, indeed, Flight Lieutenant Brian Gipson had completed two Pathfinder tours and even the passengering Flying Officer Jones had logged very nearly 1,500 hours.

The direct track from Warboys (near Huntingdon) would have taken the aircraft well south of high ground, but although cloud was known to be hanging over the hilltops the weather was generally good, and the crew decided to take in the Peak District on the way. Operationally experienced as they were, however, when cloud rose before them the decision was made to descend below it. Only this took them into the Vale of Edale, so that as they broke cloud Flight Lieutenant Gipson found himself heading into the virtually precipitous flank of Rushup Edge.

The terrain ahead

Hastily – as one might well imagine – he heaved back on the stick and powered up, managing to rear the aircraft's nose so high that, against all the odds, it flattened itself against the ground rather than driving full tilt into it. By equal good fortune there was no fire, and although all suffered injuries, everyone survived.

Retired-postman Mr Alan Chapman, of Barber Booth, recalled, 'The Oxford was like a great butterfly pinned to the hillside. To recover the engines, they only had to be rolled downhill.'

The inquiry found the pilot to blame for descending through cloud without having ascertained his position beforehand. But having directed that both he and the navigator be reproved, it was left to the officer commanding the navigational unit – with his comparatively limited powers of punishment – to administer what was, in effect, an avuncular slap on the wrist.

Impact gully, looking towards Barber Booth

VISITING THE SITE

Public parking is available in the extensive lay-by at SK 10797 84713 (250 m), just past Barber Booth. Backtracking the road for 350 yards – and under the railway bridge –, to SK 11155 84714, gives access (on the right) to the Chapel Gate track. At the sheepfold at SK 10664 84048 (1046 feet, 319 m), turning sharply left along a joining, contour-hugging path for 350 yards, will lead to a pronounced gully. The debris pool – still moderate in late 2013 – lurks in the left-hand bank 230 yards up. From here it is perfectly feasible to climb onwards, off-path, up towards Lord's Seat, to the sites there, and to the magnificent ridge walk of Rushup Edge.

Hope

5. Vickers Armstrongs Wellington Mk.3 HF613
Hope, near Castleton

SK 16179 83030 161 m

SK 15999 83418 roadside monument, A6187, Castleton Road

Unit and Station: No. 22 Operational Training Unit (OTU),

RAF Wellesbourne Mountford (east of Stratford),

No. 91 Group, Bomber Command

Date: 15 February 1943

Crew: five, all killed

- Sergeant John Douglas Kester, Royal Canadian Air Force (RCAF), pilot
- Sergeant Richard Foote Cairns, RCAF, navigator
- Sergeant Bernard Elliott Wilkinson, RCAF, bomb aimer
- Sergeant William Arthur Billy Marwood, RAF Volunteer Reserve, wireless operator/air gunner
- Sergeant William James Hackett, RCAF, air gunner

On 15 February 1943 Sergeant John Kester, of the Royal Canadian Air Force, and his mainly Canadian crew, all OTU trainees, were briefed for a solo cross-country flight from RAF Gaydon, No. 22 OTU's satellite airfield. Having only twenty hours solo on type, Sergeant Kester was specifically briefed to keep an eye out for storms, and to go round cloud build-ups rather than enter them. Just the same, at shortly after one o'clock in the afternoon, his aircraft, Wellington HF613, was heard over Hope, in Derbyshire, eighty miles north of Gaydon.

Schoolgirl Noreen Beverley, later to become Mrs Eric Robinson, had arrived home for the lunch break at a run through a sudden cloudburst. 'It was like a blizzard,' she remembered, 'violent gusts of wind, pelting snow – really awful. And then, hardly ten minutes later, there was a clear sky again.'

Mr Robinson, too, recalled the tragedy. 'We saw him coming from the Bradwell direction, and not that high above the Earles' Cement Works chimney, before we lost him in the cloud. Then we couldn't see anything for snow. Only you could tell from his engine note that he was trying to turn back.'

Except that just moments later the Wellington, its engines at high power, plummeted steeply out of the downsweeping snow flurries, struck the ground, skidded on across a ford, and exploded.

'We could see the flames from the house,' Mrs Robinson said sombrely, 'and the black smoke. But my mother wouldn't let me go over there ...'

And just as well, for as those arriving at the scene were to find, the fire had burnt fiercely, and there was nothing to be done for the crew.

It was evident that Sergeant Kester had entered what had looked like an innocuous enough cloud, not realising that a storm cell, shielded from him by the veiling stratiform layer, was just about to boil over. But although clouds, once penetrated, invariably tend to be far wider in extent than they appear on the approach, it would not have been long before the suddenly-increasing turbulence alerted him to the fact that there was more to this woolly-edged seeming-strato-cumulus than had shown itself moments earlier.

He would have had to make an instant transition onto instruments. Indeed, far more, for he was called upon to bank the unwieldy bomber hard over and then pull it around to the reverse direction as expeditiously as possible in order to regain clear sky and known terrain clearance. It would have been a lot to ask of himself even in smooth flying conditions. In the event, he found it quite beyond his capabilities, lost control, and spiralled into the ground under full power.

Although the court of inquiry did investigate the alternative possibility that ice had played its part in the loss of control, this was soon discounted. But every reporting officer up the chain was quite unequivocal in his condemnation of the conduct of the flight.

The unit's commanding officer pointedly proffered his own briefing forbidding the pilot to, 'enter heavy squalls or showers, but to avoid them'.

At best a rather impracticable authorisation under which to dispatch an inexperienced Canadian crew on a lively mid-February English day.

For his part the station commander fumed, and scribbled, 'Disobedience or disregard of orders in entering a cloud'. *A* cloud! While the chief instructor commented testily, 'This form of disregard of orders is frequent'. And from their cerulean heights both the Air Officer Commanding, and the Air Officer Commanding-in-Chief concurred.

A savage condemnation, surely! Of an inexperienced pilot who had clearly been taken unawares by the ferocity of a localised storm. Yet, there is the larger picture to be taken into consideration.

By the time No. 22 Operational Training Unit was disbanded on 25 July 1945 it had trained 9,000 aircrew; indeed, at its peak, in 1944, it was turning out 113 operationally-ready crews a month. But this was never to be without a cost, and between Wellesbourne Mountford and Gaydon the training cost was high, with 315 aircrew killed, 80 injured, and 96 Wellingtons lost.

So perhaps it is understandable that while living with such losses took its toll upon the nerves of the aircrew and ground personnel, it wore equally, at least, upon those of the senior officers responsible for producing the crews so desperately needed. Remembering too, that each of the 9,000 aircrew trained was a volunteer. Additionally, that nearly all were very young, and it could be, to an above-the-average degree imbued with all the impetuously adventurous qualities engendered, not only by their own years, but of the tumultuous times they were living through.

Accepting this, it can be appreciated that to condone an apparent shortfall in discipline might well have led to even higher casualty rates. In which context the severity of the report into the loss of just one of the ninety-six aircraft, Wellington HF613, might become a little more palatable. Notwithstanding that the individual human hurt remains. But at least it can be measured against the overall human cost at stake.

As for Wellington HF613, it had impacted into a field just short of the northern bank of Peakshole Water – even then, locally known as 'The Styx'! – and disintegrated as it ground its way across the stream and up the slope beyond.

Mr Robert Stamper, of Hathersage, arrived early. 'Aside from the wheels in the stream,' he said, 'there was nothing that looked like an aeroplane.'

Yet the scars soon healed, stock continued to drink at the ford, and picnics were enjoyed on the banks. Until 4 April 1982 when a walker discovered two badly corroded and potentially-lethal practice bombs!

In the interim, researcher Mr Stephen Lewis had been instrumental in having Sergeant Bernard Wilkinson's sister visit from Canada, and in due course Mr Robinson had a wall plaque set on the Castleton Road looking across to the crash site. Only yards, in fact, from the Canadian Maple, planted on that visit as a tribute to the memory of 'Bunny', the erstwhile bomb aimer of Wellington HF613.

Regarding the cement-factory chimney, Mrs Margaret Brown (née Dakin), who grew up in the Hope Valley, remembered a broadcast made by Lord Haw Haw, William Joyce, the American born, Irish nurtured, English traitor who spewed propaganda from Germany and was eventually hanged. 'You people in the Hope Valley', he goaded, 'think you are so snug and safe. But the moment we cross the coast we can see the smoke from the Earle's chimney.' Mrs Brown smiled, 'We were quite literally petrified. So we switched off the radio at once, scarcely daring to move or make a noise.'

Terminal site, on the slope beyond Peakshole Water, from the initial impact area

Debris from the impact area

The tasteful memorial plaque commissioned by Mr Eric Robinson

VISITING THE SITE

Opportunity town parking is available at both ends of the southerly-looping footpath so pleasantly connecting Hope and Castleton. At SK 16246 82969 (180 m) the terminal site is just yards downslope towards the ford, while recently emerged metal scraps might be found in the nearest drystone wall. The memorial plaque on the busy A6187, Castleton Road, is also worth (carefully) pausing for.

Moscar Moor

6. De Havilland Vampire T.11 XE866
Crow Chin, Stanage Edge

SK 22437 85694 427 m

Unit and Station: No. 4 Flying Training School, RAF Worksop,
No. 23 Group, Flying Training Command

Date: 8 August 1957

Crew: pilots, two, both killed

- Flying Officer Phillip Redvers Jones, instructor
- Flying Officer Derek John Brett, pupil pilot

The de Havilland Vampire dual-seat, T.11 ('Tee Eleven') could not only change altitude more swiftly than any previous RAF trainer but also, being jet propelled, more smoothly. Unfortunately, the Vampire's Mark 14 altimeter could make a problem of this otherwise desirable characteristic.

Ten-of-thousands of feet needle: very easily missed, especially behind other needles, and in a poorly lit cockpit.

Barometric sub-scale: very easy to set an incorrect setting

The Mk.14 Pressure Altimeter. By 1959, just two years later, the RAF **Flying Manual, AP129,** *would actually warn of the unsuitability for jet operations of both the tens-of-thousands of feet needle and the barometric sub-scale*

The trouble lay with the presentation. For while a long pointer indicated hundreds of feet and an intermediate one, thousands, the tens-of-thousands pointer was miniscule and only too easy to overlook. Certainly, it was so common for a student pilot to be 10,000 feet lower than he thought he was that, just as he was about to commence a rapid descent, the fiendish instructor would gleefully whip off the instrument-flying hood – to reveal treetops flashing past the canopy! But it was just as common for a student to be sitting at 10,000 feet while believing himself to be at just 1,000 feet above the ground, when the fiend would leave the hapless one hooded, but take control, roll the aircraft onto its back – and pull towards the ground in a near-vertical dive. It really was that easy to misread the Mk.14 altimeter!

And T.11 XE866 was so equipped on 8 August 1957 when flown by Worksop instructor Flying Officer Phillip Jones and his pupil, Flying Officer Derek Brett.

Initially they investigated the effects of high altitude on handling. This, an absorbing session of manoeuvring at various speeds, concluded with a protracted dive to demonstrate high-speed effects. The main concerns throughout this dive were to prevent the nose coming up (the more the speed increased the more it wanted to), and to maintain a hawk-eyed lookout for other aircraft, twin occupations which vied to take the attention from the height being so rapidly reeled away!

All that done, it would be time to level off, to re-check the stability of the gyroscopically-controlled instruments, and to prepare for the recovery to base. Only it was absolutely crucial that the height read off the altimeter was checked – and double checked. For although the ground controller did all the timing and direction-finding during the recovery, the pilot simply obeying instructions, the controller relied upon him to report the aircraft's height.

There were two types of recovery, one begun at high level, 20,000 feet, the other at medium level, 10,000 feet. In the descent from a high-level recovery, the pilot would advise the controller that he was 'approaching 6,000 feet and turning inbound', but would continue the descent as he did so. In a medium-level recovery he would call the height, but would level off and slow down as he turned, continuing the descent only when heading towards the airfield. Flying Officer Jones had elected to carry out the medium-level procedure so he duly reported 6,000 feet – and was presumed to have levelled off. Except that only moments later he flew into the ground at high speed, the Vampire careering across flat moorland to catastrophically strike the vertical face of Stanage Edge at Crow Chin. The aircraft exploded, and neither occupant survived.

The board of inquiry ('board', now, in 1951, no longer 'court'! – similarly, pupil pilots had become student pilots!) while precisely costing out the accident at £73,801 for crew and aircraft, made two, not exclusive, submissions. The first was that Flying Officer Jones had mistaken the type of controlled descent he was engaged in, and instead of levelling out at 6,000 feet, had continued the descent unabated, flying into the ground in a port bank only half way around the inbound turn. The second submission was that the altimeter had been misread, and that he had started the procedure 10,000 feet too low.

It really was that easy – and that common – to misread the Mk.14 family of altimeters.

VISITING THE SITE

Stanage Edge, a Mecca for climbers but a great ridge walk too, is well supplied with parking places; additionally, there is restricted lay-by parking on the A57 at SK 22984 87850. However, although contemporary newspaper photographs showed widely-scattered debris draping the cliff, the initial impact point, below Crow Chin, is now in thick heather, while only scraps are likely to be found among the rocks; the case, certainly, in mid 2013.

From the impact site, looking towards Crow Chin

The terminal site

A retaining bracket for an undercarriage-door, found amid the rocks in 2004. Having this identified by the (de Havilland) Mosquito Trust discomfited the author, who had hitherto believed the Vampires he flew to have been made of comfortingly solid metal

Sheffield

7. Boeing B-17G (Flying Fortress) 42-31322 '*Mi Amigo*'
Endcliffe Park, Sheffield

SK 32857 85899 138 m
Unit and Station: United States Eighth Army Air Force,
305th Bombardment Group, 364th Bombardment Squadron,
AAF105 (RAF Chelveston), south-east of Kettering
Date: 22 February 1944
Crew: ten, United States Army Air Force, all killed

- First Lieutenant John Glennon Krieghauser, pilot
- Second Lieutenant Lyle J. Curtis, co-pilot
- Second Lieutenant John W. Humphrey, navigator
- Second Lieutenant Melchor Hernandez, bombardier
- Staff Sergeant Robert E. Mayfield, radio operator
- Staff Sergeant Harry W. Estabrooks, engineer/top turret gunner
- Sergeant Charles H. Tuttle, ball-turret gunner
- Sergeant Maurice O. Robbins, tail gunner
- Sergeant Vito R. Ambrosio, right waist gunner
- Master Sergeant George U. Williams, left waist gunner

On the 22 February 1944 First Lieutenant John Krieghauser's aircraft, B-17 (Flying Fortress), 42-31322, '*Mi Amigo*', was one of a force dispatched to bomb Ålborg airfield in Denmark. Finding the target obscured by cloud, however, the raiders turned back, only to meet strong fighter opposition during which '*Mi Amigo*' was seen to suffer damage to its fuselage and engines. It then fell out of formation, and subsequently jettisoned its bombs into the North Sea.

When next seen it was circling Sheffield, some eighty miles north-west of its Northamptonshire base. Then, as an engine cut, auto-rotation first rolled, then spiralled, it into a Sheffield park. Just one airman survived the impact, poignantly pleading with a young boy, 'Can you save me, Kid?' only to be engulfed in the conflagration moments later.

It is not known why First Lieutenant Krieghauser did not order the crew to abandon the aircraft before the situation became critical. Having suffered battle damage, though, it is probable that he had casualties on board who could not jump.

The investigation established beyond doubt that the aircraft had been totally out of control when it crashed. Yet the citations for First Lieutenant Krieghauser's posthumous Distinguished Flying Cross and his Air Medal with Oak Leaf Cluster both speak of his avoiding 'an English home' by manoeuvring 'the crippled aeroplane over the dwelling'. Which seems a shame, for he and his crew deserve much better than such patent glosses, as do the other 420 American aircrew! and the other forty-two American heavy bombers! lost over Europe that day.

Perhaps, though, their memory has been better served by the memorial erected in 1969; by the ten American oaks fringing the riverside knoll; and by the annual homage paid to them and to all American aircrew who died while operating from British airfields in the course of the Second World War.

The memorial

Memorial detail

VISITING THE SITE

The monument at Endcliffe Park, erected on the crash site, has very fittingly become a focus for both pilgrimage and reflection. For not only was the Flying Fortress one of the very few aircraft to crash in the High Peak due to battle damage, there is the additional wonder that it did not fall on a built-up area.

8. Gloster Meteor Mk.8 WB108
Treeton Colliery, Rotherham

SK 43746 88039 74 m impact point
SK 43602 87820 68 m pit reservoir terminal point
Unit and Station: No. 211 Flying Training School, RAF Worksop, No. 25 Group, Flying Training Command
Date: 21 December 1954
Crew: pilot, pupil pilot, killed
• Pilot Officer Douglas Gibson Edwards

On 21 December 1954 pupil pilot, Pilot Officer Douglas Edwards, was tasked for a solo general-handling flight. Twenty-three minutes after take-off, however, he lost control and crashed onto a colliery spoil tip at Treeton, Rotherham.

Pilot Officer Edwards had logged 22 hours on the twin-jet Meteor, eight of them solo. He had also gained a White instrument-flying rating, showing his competence. In view of this, when seeking the cause of the crash, the investigation discounted disorientation, settling instead upon a loss of radio contact, together with a possible misreading of his altimeter.

It was apparent that, having initially steered westwards, Pilot Officer Edwards had found the cloud too thick for him to carry out any upper-air work. Accordingly, in order to descend safely, he homed back to Worksop by obtaining a series of 'steers' – headings to fly – from the tower. Having arrived overhead, and knowing the local safety height, he then commenced a free let-down. After which no other transmission was received from him.

It was later established that the heading Pilot Officer Edwards had chosen for his descent had taken him into Rotherham's industrial haze – in those days a perennial condition. In a reasoned attempt to combat the poor visibility as he tried to establish his position, he had both lowered one-third flap and extended his airbrakes.

Holding level flight with the flap meant lowering the Meteor's nose. The flap also allowed him to fly more slowly. Flying level with the airbrakes extended necessitated him increasing power. But whereas 'Power against brake' is an anathema in piston-engined handling, it is a useful tool in jet handling, jet engines being characteristically slow to wind up from low power to high power. Using airbrakes, therefore, gave him almost immediate engine response.

His preparation showed wisdom beyond his experience. Unfortunately, having levelled, he found himself facing a steep hill. Thanks to his foresight, powering up was no problem, but the zoom climb required proved too much for the Meteor. Either he ran it out of airspeed and stalled, or, in pulling too hard, he entered a 'g' – or high speed – stall.

Whichever one is academic, for witnesses saw him appear through the murk in a descending right-hand turn, hurriedly level his wings and raise the nose, but only just clear the crest of Spa Hill before his aircraft sank markedly. They then saw it strike the spoil tip beyond, cartwheel, and explode.

The wreckage spill was widespread, with at least one engine hurtling downslope to land in the colliery reservoir. Mrs Dorothy Stevenson, whose husband was a surface worker at the Treeton Pit, remembered, 'I saw this aeroplane appear. Then it disappeared below my line of sight and exploded in Tip Field. All I could think of was, "Who is at work above ground today?"' Fortuitously, no colliery workers were hurt.

Mrs Pat Nuthall, also of Treeton, was at her bedroom window. 'I retain this impression,' she recalled, 'of seeing the plane an instant before it hit. It struck the hill, and there was this cloud of black smoke and fierce flames. It was horrible, for though there must have been someone in it, nobody could have survived.'

As late as 1976 components and debris were being unearthed, notably from the pit reservoir, but then the colliery closed, housing estates burgeoning in its place. Even before that, in the wake of the 1966 Aberfan disaster, the spoil heap had been flattened.

The impact point, looking towards Treeton

Treeton Colliery, and the pit reservoir, 1941

Photo-match of the 1941 scene, with Cannonthorpe Rise replacing the pit reservoir

Back in 1954 the investigation had submitted that the crash had been caused by an error of judgement, albeit due to inexperience. It was clear, however, that Pilot Officer Edwards had been shocked to find himself so close to the ground; accordingly, it was recommended that the replacement of the easy-to-misread Mk.14 altimeter variant, a measure subsequently adopted.

It was only to be expected, perhaps, that fables would attach themselves to a crash which happened so close to a populated area. But it is unfortunate, perhaps, that these held sway in 2005 when a consensus was held to name the fast-maturing amenity which the spoil heap had become.

Among contenders were what seemed to be the eminently fitting 'Colliers' Crest', suggested by crash-witness Mrs Nuthall – 'built by generations of miners, so commemorating miners.' The title chosen, however, was 'The Edwards Meteor Way,' with the local news-sheet enthusing, 'The brave pilot crashed into the tip after circling the village a number of times to avoid hitting homes and causing civilian casualties.' Unfortunate, because while cold-shouldering the very real bravery of untold generations of Treeton miners, such a fallacious gloss does no service to the cause of flight safety, the cause which the hapless Pilot Officer Edwards so tragically furthered.

VISITING THE SITE

This crash site, with opportunity parking at SK 43518 87937, may not present itself as a natural venue for even suburban-tied walkers, but it is one which nowadays affords both a superb overview of the area's rich tradition of industry and a pleasing panorama embracing the built-up areas, the parks, and the distant upland moors.

Ringinglow

9. Vickers Armstrongs Wellington Mk.1C Z8980
Burbage Moor, Rud Hill

SK 26149 83798 414 m

Unit and Station: No. 27 Operational Training Unit, RAF Lichfield,
No. 91 Group, Bomber Command

Date 17: July 1942

Crew: five, all injured

- Sergeant Thomas Frank Thompson, Royal Australian Air Force (RAAF), pilot
- Pilot Officer J.W. Moore, navigator
- Sergeant J.H. Levett, wireless operator/air gunner
- Sergeant Kennington John Hythe Harris, RAAF, air gunner
- Sergeant Jacob Henry Roden, RAAF, rear gunner

On 17 July 1942, in the course of a night cross-country exercise from Lichfield, Thomas Frank Thompson and his largely Australian trainee crew made a significant navigational error when, peering down at blacked-out Nottingham, they mistook it for Leicester. This was not a surprising mistake considering their unfamiliarity with the United Kingdom's urban sprawl. However, it caused them to believe they were twenty-three miles south of where they actually were, and therefore, over low-lying ground. Accordingly, when they tried to edge under cloud with 1,450 feet on their altimeter, they flew into 1,400 feet-above-sea-level Burbage Moor.

The Wellington, sturdy though it was, splayed across the moor, and burst into flames. Notwithstanding which all five crew members were able to get clear, although Sergeant Thomas, the pilot, had suffered a significant head injury, rear-gunner Sergeant Jacob Roden had sustained a broken leg, and the others had less serious injuries.

Fortunately some members of the Home Guard arrived and were accredited with actually pulling some crew members clear of the flames! Then, having escorted the still-mobile survivors to the road, they constructed makeshift stretchers for the non-walking casualties. Gratifyingly, their senior NCO, a Sergeant Lowey, received a well-deserved King's Commendation on their behalf.

The court of inquiry decided that a snap navigational judgement had been rashly made, and indicted the crew for overconfidence.

Because of their diverse injuries, the men were unable to complete the course together, and as each became fit, so he joined a fresh crew, their subsequent careers serving as a salutary reminder that, high as attrition rates were among trainee crews, they were even higher once training gave place to operations.

So, air-gunner Sergeant Kennington Harris was to be killed raiding Essen in January 1943 when a night-fighter downed his Lancaster. Rear-gunner Sergeant Roden was killed in a Wellington in September 1942, and Sergeant Thompson in August 1944. A compelling rate of wastage – of sacrifice.

The debris pool in 2013, looking towards Upper Burbage Bridge

VISITING THE SITE

Extensive parking is available at Upper Burbage Bridge. Setting course from the road at SK 25912 83021, it is best to expect a half-mile off-path trek across bog, hummock grass, and heather. Probably the best scheme is to head on 001°M towards the un-named mere at SK 25953 83876 – an exclusive picnic spot! –, then turn right on 116°M for 230 yards to reach the site. To return in poor visibility, the road at Upper Burbage forms a safe backstop to any southerly heading. In early 2013 there was still a patch of burnt ground strewn with fragments of molten metal. Yet it might be necessary to cast about to find the spot (Scornful sheep, who know where it is, should be ignored during the process).

Foolow

10. Avro Shackleton MR [maritime reconnaissance] Mk.3 (prototype) WR970
Foolow, north-east of Tideswell

SK 19331 76643 275 m

Operator: A.V. Roe and Co. Ltd., Stockport

Date: 7 December 1956

Crew: four, all killed

- Squadron Leader Jack Bertram Wales, OBE, DFC (A.V. Roe test pilot)
- George Alan Blake, flight engineer
- Charles O'Neill, technical observer
- Roy Greenhaigh, technical observer

Shackleton WR970, courtesy of Kenneth Munson

The Second World War proved both the efficacy of, and the necessity for, an efficient maritime reconnaissance patrol aircraft. As a result the Avro Shackleton was developed to replace the Lancaster in that role. Always deemed pleasant to fly, the type was constantly being updated, the modifications invariably increasing both weight and dimensions. So it was that in September 1955, when the tricycle-undercarriaged Mark 3 version was first flown, considerable testing was called for. Indeed, it was not until a full year after it first flew that the Mark 3 prototype, WR970, was handed to The Aeroplane and Armament Experimental Establishment (A&AEE) at Boscombe Down for additional testing. Then, on the 28 November 1956, it was returned to Avro's Woodford plant, near Stockport, for further stall-warning development tests. It was in the course of these that it crashed at Foolow, in Derbyshire, narrowly missing the village, but killing all on board.

The scene at Foolow, courtesy **Derby Evening Telegraph**

*A **confirmatory debris search at Foolow***

Crashing within the bounds of the village as it did, meant that there were many witnesses; in particular a former RAF flight engineer who was to recall that as the aircraft broke cloud it was spiralling, and doing no more than 60 knots. From which he deduced that it had been locked into some form of deep stall.

Another witness was the then-farmworking teenager Mr Les Bond, years later to return to become the landlord of the village's Bull's Head pub. In 1956, looking up from his mucking out, and shocked at seeing the machine flying so low and in such obvious difficulties, he had screamed out, 'Get up, you bugger! You're going to crash!'

Then, as he explained, when the worst happened, he had run to the scene. 'On the way I overtook Frank Harrison –' He paused, and suddenly smiled. 'He was carrying a little fire extinguisher, although what good he thought that would do.' Then abruptly, he sobered. 'But he did find a use for it. For when he caught up with me I'd come to one of the crew. There was nothing left of his clothing, and although Frank played the extinguisher on him we were far too late. All we could do was cover him up.' Again he reflected. 'There was so little to be done, that after a while I just went back to my mucking out.'

But he remembered too, later that evening, sitting at home listening to the wireless, scarcely able to credit that the august BBC could get so many things so wrong.

The official inquiry was able to substantiate much of what the witnesses – if not the BBC – had reported. The testing, it seems, had reached the stage of examining the stalling characteristics of the aircraft in the attack configuration – bomb bays open and radar scanner extended. It appears that, in the course of this, a level turn was commenced and the speed reduced towards the stall. Except that, as on a previous occasion at Boscombe Down, and as witnessed now by the crew of a coincidentally passing Lincoln bomber, the aircraft rolled markedly, then fell away into a spin. In this case, however, its rotational dive took it into thick cloud!

Subsequent examination of the engines showed that during its passage through the cloud the Shackleton had actually become inverted, spinning belly up for some time before righting itself just before it emerged from cloud to end its fatal fall.

One witness, however, Mr John Hancock, might have been able to put the investigators on the track of this rather earlier, had he been interviewed. 'I was at Shepherd's Park Farm,' he recounted, 'just to the north of the village, when I heard this noise of aero engines hunting up and down – trying to break the stall, as I thought later. Then the aircraft appeared out of the clouds at about a thousand feet, between me and the village. I've always fancied that the first thing to appear was the tail plane. But then the whole machine fell from the cloud with one wing hard down, and that was the way it hit the ground.' He went on, 'I rushed over in my car. To find that, although the heat was intense, the aircraft wasn't all burning, for some of the crew members had been thrown clear: I remember one was wearing an Irving flying jacket. – But there was nothing to be done for any of them.'

VISITING THE SITE

This site is included in the debris section by virtue of the fact that a temporary plaque was once placed on the war-memorial site, so possibly it will be replaced. Certainly, there is debris to be found, but below the cropped-turf surface of the drystone-walled enclosures where WR970 spiralled itself into the ground. Debris or not, though, this archetypically-English village repays a reflective visit for any number of reasons.

Dronfield

11. Gloster Meteor TMk.8 WE904
Millthorpe (south-west of Dronfield)

SK 31722 76331 141 m
Unit and Station: No. 211 Flying Training School, RAF Worksop,
No. 25 Group, Flying Training Command
Date: 12 May 1955
Crew: pilot: killed
• Pilot Officer Robert Anthony Tritton

When Pilot Officer Robert Tritton was briefed by his instructor to carry out a solo medium-level exercise in the course of which he would practise the 'Homing and Controlled-Descent through Cloud' recovery procedure, he had not yet taken a formal instrument-rating test on jet trainers. He was told, therefore, to steer clear of actual cloud.

At that time this recovery procedure was the most common method of safely bringing an aircraft down through cloud, a ground controller using direction-finding equipment telling the pilot what to do, the pilot simply following instructions. In carrying it out, the aircraft would first be homed to the overhead, then turned onto a safe heading and descended, initially away from the airfield. Next, roughly halfway through the descent, it would be turned inbound again, continuing its descent until it broke cloud and the pilot declared that he could see the airfield.

The long-titled procedure was more succinctly known as a 'QGH', the tri-letter group being one of aviation's several survivors from the 'Q' brevity-code employed when most airborne communication was by the ploddingly-protracted morse code. There were, however, two distinct types of QGH, a high-level, starting at 20,000 feet, and a medium-level procedure. Pilot Officer Tritton had been briefed to practise the medium-level approach, starting at 10,000 feet.

After take-off he elected to clear from the airfield in a westerly climb.

The next call to be expected from him would have been his declaration that he was at 10,000 feet and requesting a QGH. However, six minutes after departure he transmitted instead, the confirmatory safety call, 'Oxygen checked', a necessary advisory with jet aircraft climbing so swiftly, but only required when climbing through twenty-thousand feet to a higher level.

Nobody in the control tower, not even the duty instructor, would necessarily have been aware that the pupil's briefing had called for a 10,000 foot commencement clear of cloud. There was upper cloud, however, and just seven minutes after take-off, Pilot Officer Tritton's machine dived vertically into the ground and exploded, killing him instantly.

The cause of crash had to be matter of speculation, but witnesses had seen the aircraft emerge from cloud in a near-vertical dive, then recover somewhat, only to roll into a steeply banked turn and crash. The board found, therefore, that Pilot Officer Tritton had entered cloud at high level, become disorientated, and lost control, thereafter entering a near-vertical dive from which, due to inexperience, he had been unable to recover.

Then, however, they rather harshly plumped for condemnation, recording that in climbing above his briefed height the pupil had disobeyed instructions. And yet he had faithfully transmitted his safety call, in effect, openly declaring that he was climbing through 20,000 feet: rather the action of a pupil who had mistaken the type of QGH to be flown rather than one deliberately flouting his briefed instructions!

What did emerge was that Pilot Officer Tritton's solo flying had exceeded his dual – that is, his supervised – flights by what was now seen as far too great a margin. It was also observed that too little time had been devoted to instrument flying. Presumably these aspects of training, by which pupils were put at unnecessary risk through insufficient supervision and instruction, were promptly addressed.

In crashing, the aircraft had dived vertically into a barn adjacent to Brookside Farm, just north of the ford, in the village of Millthorpe. As the farm's incumbent, Mr John Knight, attested, he had heard the aircraft pass above him, 'Its engines sounding odd', but then almost at once approach again.

'I was just leading my toddler son into the barn,' he recalled, 'and had just reached up to push the door inwards when, suddenly, there was no barn, just the door, and the stone surround! Behind me, the house roof had mostly gone, while the other barns were wrecked and roofless. And John and I were just left there, with not a mark on us.'

Mr John Knight, at the impact point,
showing how he opened the then barn

Evidently the Meteor had buried itself so deeply that the explosion had initially been contained at low level. But as the blast had then surged outwards over Mr Knight's head not a structure in the immediate vicinity had escaped! Rotating components from the engines had also sprung from the crater, one embedding itself in a tree trunk, another striking and decapitating a tree top before burying itself in a meadow 400 yards off, with a third scything its way through both walls of a second stone barn to fall just short of the main road.

A compressor embedded in a tree

Another former barn, pierced by a turbine

Mr Knight smiled. 'As the roof of a cowshed was blown off the main supporting beam fell across the brick-built separating compartments, but we found that each cow had simply lowered its back.'

He recalled too the RAF assessor ('They were all charming people'), on the spot within two hours, even amid the chaos pressing him for his estimate of the damage; and officialdom subsequently refusing to pay for re-building in stone, but only in the cheaper brick. Then there was the RAF salvage crew. 'They loaded the debris into this vehicle they called a "Queen Mary" which completely filled the road! But people were picking up metal – aluminium, I suppose – for years afterwards.'

Sobering, he recalled also, the visit by the trainee-pilot's relatives ...

VISITING THE SITE

By 2014 Brookside Farm, where the barn stood, had long become a private property, and even the trees bore only muted scars. But a village group had positioned a memorial to the hapless Pilot Officer Tritton adjacent to the village well-dressing site, even if choosing to give most prominence to the date of their own involvement, fifty years on.

Erected by the residents of
Millthorpe and Holmesfield
12th May 2005
Commemorating the
50th anniversary of
a tragic plane crash
At 3.25pm on 12th May 1955,
Gloster Meteor F8 WE904
crashed close to this site
The 19 year old pilot was the only fatality

In memory of
Pilot Officer Robert A. Tritton
of Stonehouse, Gloucestershire
211 FTS, RAF Worksop
"Forever with the Lord"

The memorial plaque, revealing the priorities afforded

12. McDonnell Douglas Phantom RF-4C 64-1018
Rose Wood, Unthank, near Chesterfield

SK 31062 75722 187 m impact crater
SK 25630 75250 pilot landed
SK 25720 75310 navigator landed
Unit and Squadron: United States Air Force in Europe, 3rd Air Force,
10th Tactical Reconnaissance Wing,
1st Tactical Reconnaissance Squadron, RAF Alconbury, Huntingdon
Date: 6 May 1970
Crew: two, ejected, one with a serious injury:
- Major Donald Eugene Tokar, United States Air Force, pilot, smashed thigh
- Major Peter Martin Dunn, USAF, navigator

The McDonnell Douglas Phantom RF-4C was the unarmed photographic-reconnaissance version of the Phantom F-4C fighter, but although the Phantom's sheer nippiness had got it out of many scrapes, notably in Vietnam where, it is held, none were shot down by other aircraft, successful evasion by the unarmed version called for the adoption of extreme tactics, tactics which sometimes required the aircraft to be placed in equally extreme attitudes.

It was necessary, of course, for such manoeuvres to be practised, and this was the purpose of the sortie upon which Major Donald Tokar and Major Peter Dunn, his navigator, embarked on 6 May 1970. The exercise was to be carried out in combination with another Phantom, one attacking, the other evading. Initially, only mild zooming and rolling evolutions were flown. Then, with sufficient fuel burned off – and, therefore, with the machines that much lighter – the pair turned to steeper and faster manoeuvres. This incremental approach was adopted because, the sortie being non-operational, safety was paramount; so much so that loss-of-control recovery techniques, even to the extent of streaming the drag parachute in flight! had been particularly stressed at the pre-flight briefing.

Just as well, for forty-four minutes into the sortie Major Tokar, in seeking to recover from a steep dive ('low-nose, high speed maneuver'), found that his controls were not answering.

The subsequent investigation would focus upon the position of the moveable-tailplane assembly, but at the time it was sufficient for the two crew – each having around three thousand hours of flying experience – to know that the situation was beyond recovery. Accordingly, on Major Tokar's order, both ejected safely, landing on Curbar Edge. Major Dunn came down lightly, albeit suffering abrasions when he was dragged by his parachute, but Major Tokar, landing among rocks, smashed his thigh.

The section of Curbar Edge upon which the crew landed

Major Tokay being stretchered down, **Sheffield Morning Telegraph**

July 1970, Appreciation being shown at RAF Lakenheath. Left to right: Councillor Ken Adlington, Major Tokar, Police Constable Charlesworth, Andrew Adlington (in the Martin Baker ejection seat), Major Dunn, Brian Whittaker, and Dr Dalrymple Smith. Courtesy of **The Derbyshire Times**

Farmer Ken Adlington, latterly of Curbar, lived in Warren Lodge, just below Curbar Edge, at the time. 'As I drove home,' he recalled, 'I saw the parachutes. One of these – the navigator's – was hanging over the Edge. Having raised the alarm, I climbed up with Brian Whittaker, Police Constable Charlesworth, and a few more locals, to find that the other American had fallen among the rocks and broken his leg.' He smiled. 'Once we'd got the navigator off the cliff he began telling us how grateful he was for his English-made ejection seat. He told us too, that as they'd been coming down the pilot had pointed at Barbrook Reservoir and then to the rocks, and called across, "Well, that's it. We're either going to drown or get smashed on the rocks." Anyway, we got them both down to more level ground where Dr Dalrymple Smith and the ambulance crews tended them until, about half an hour later, an RAF helicopter arrived and lifted them both away.'

Just a week after the crash Major Dunn, the uninjured navigator, wrote a general letter of appreciation to the local newspaper thanking all the Curbar villagers for their assistance, making particular note of one act of kindness. 'A wonderful gentleman named Mr Village,' he wrote, 'even made a quick trip home and came back with a bottle of brandy – I've never had a more enjoyable tot.' And three months later, with Major Tokar still on crutches after two months in traction, the pair entertained villagers from both Curbar and Millthorpe, at their Lakenheath base.

From Millthorpe, because the abandoned Phantom had come down at that village's Unthank Lane Farm, just inside the adjoining Rose Wood, diving almost vertically into the ground and creating a wide, deep crater. Mr Ian Biggin, a son of the owner, recalled, 'I was working nearby when I heard this aircraft diving, and then saw it plummet into the wood. A massive mushroom cloud went up, with debris flying everywhere, and then, for a long time after everything else had settled, streams of film began descending, much wider than 35 mm cine film, and much of it alight. But moments after the explosion another Phantom appeared, roaring past, virtually scraping the woods, evidently trying to see what had happened.'

'Ah! didn't it,' Ian's father, Neville, confirmed. 'I was in the barn, and following so close after the explosion I thought it was the crashed one bouncing my way, so I dived into the hay.'

'Extreme low flying was something we got used to while the Americans were on site,' said Neville's other son, Stewart, 'We'd never seen anything like it. In fact, they set up a caravan just beyond the road corner and when a bigwig came in his helicopter some days later another Phantom very nearly crashed into it. Indeed, we heard them on the radio ordering him to 'Get his arse out of here', or suchlike. But minutes later he came screaming down the wood again – multiple airshows every day, it was!'

'The whole thing,' Neville agreed, 'was incredible from the start. Lakenheath, their main base, is about a hundred miles away, yet after the crash some Americans were here within an hour! In great high wheeled vehicles! And eventually they'd coach in 60 or 70 black airmen every day, putting bits in plastic bags.' He paused. 'As for damage, there was a hole in the barn roof, and another in the house, near the weather vane; and the undercarriage had caught a field hedge. Then there was a great tree, blown up by the roots, just outside, and clods of earth everywhere – one fell on a wheelbarrow which our chap had only left moments before, enough to overfill both it and him. So it was clear there'd have to be some compensation. Then I remembered that a tumbled forty-yard stretch of wall ran from just near the crater, and thought I might get a new one out of them.' He grinned ruefully. 'But of course, that particular Phantom squadron's job was aerial reconnaissance, and all they did was send me a photograph of the area, taken before the crash, showing the wall already flat!'

Son Ian, displayed a box full of fragments, including the aircraft's radar altimeter. This is a 'second generation' height-reading device which, by bouncing signals off the earth, gives the aircraft a true indication of its height above the terrain directly beneath it. A device, that is, that could have saved a great number of the aircraft covered in this series! 'I've also got the cockpit clock,' Ian said, 'stopped at the moment of impact.'

Ian's brother, Stewart, pointed out where a great chunk of debris had come through the barn roof, explaining then, 'But over in the wood where the plane itself landed, it had always been marshy, and although they brought in a massive great digger, in the end, they gave up trying to get up the rest, and backfilled the hole.'

When researching the site, copious fragmented-airframe parts were discovered just beneath the surface, many in an advanced state of corrosion quite unlike that normally found with debris from earlier, particularly Second World War, crash sites. The built-in redundancy of the times, perhaps? Although a more striking sign of changed times would be to compare the relative experience of the Phantom aircrew involved, with the lack of it among aircrew of earlier years, the Phantom pilot, with 3,000 hours, having fourteen years of Service flying behind him, rather than the four or five years and the 700 or so hours of the majority of his World War Two forebears.

Phantom impact crater

Debris from the crater area

The radar altimeter. Whereas the pressure altimeter is merely a barometer calibrated to indicate height above any set datum, pulses from the radar altimeter show the true height above the terrain directly below. During the war years such an altimeter could have saved scores of lives over Peakland

VISITING THE SITE

Courtesy aside, considering the family's evident interest, it would clearly repay any visitor to make contact before viewing the site. But, having left the road at SK 30934 76093, where there is opportunity parking, a public footpath does lead the 440 yards to the crater. The crater – or hollow, rather – is immediately inside Rose Wood, just beyond the junction of footpath and bridleway, and may well be covered with brambles. Yet odd scraps of surface debris are still to be found among the dead leaves.

Stockport

13. Canadair Argonaut C-4, G-ALHG
Stockport

SJ 89896 90076 61 m
Operator: British Midland Airways, Castle Donington, Derby
Date: 4 June 1967
Occupants: seventy-two passengers and two crew members died. Thirteen persons survived.
Crew:
- Captain Harry Marlow, survived
- First Officer Christopher Pollard, killed
- Flight Engineer Gerald Lloyd, killed
- Stewardess Miss Julia Partleton, survived
- Steward Tony Taylor, survived

Passengers: (Official list; but sources vary). These were killed:
Mrs Dorothy Ackroyd; Mr and Mrs Ayland; Mr William and Mrs Eliza Booth; Mrs Catherine Brooks; Mr Herbert, Mrs Phyllis, and Miss Christine Denton; Mr Ronald and Mrs Annie Cowgill; Mr Philip Cruse; Mr Bernard and Mrs Jane Down; Mrs C Gill; Mrs Goodwin; Mr and Mrs Harland; Mr Alan and Mrs Kathleen Hughes; Mrs Elsie James; Mr Arthur and Mrs Elsie Kemp; Mr Roy Latham and Mrs Margaret Latham; Miss Mabel Mellor; Mrs and Miss Nolan; Mrs Owen; Mr and Mrs Reynolds; Mr, Mrs, Master and infant Shaw; Mr Harry, Mrs Joan and Master John Stansfield; Mr and Mrs Smart; Mr Brian and Mrs Ann Stott; Mr Alec and Mrs Gwen Smith; Mr and Mrs Arthur Smith and Master David Smith; Mrs Taylor; Mr Royston and Mrs Nancy Taylor; Mr Mrs Raymond Tomlinson, and Master Michael and Miss Ann Tomlinson; Mr Phillip, Mrs Jean and Master Thorne; Mr Thomas, Mrs Jean, Master William and Miss Jeanette Walsh; Mrs and Master Williams; Mr Ivan and Mrs Marjorie, and Miss Wilshaw; Miss Joan Wood; Mr Ruben and Mrs Sonia Woolfson; Mr and Mrs Joseph Nicholson;

Mr Alan and Mrs Jean Taylor; Mr Raymond; Frank Thompson; Mrs Phyllis Elsie Thompson.

These survived:
Miss Fiona Child; Miss Mary Green; Miss Susan Howarth; Mr Allan Kee Johnson; Mr Albert Owen; Miss Lilly Parry; Mr David Ralphs; Miss Vivian Werrett; Master Billy and Master Harold Wood.

The tail section, courtesy of the **Stockport Express**

On 4 June 1967 Argonaut G-ALHG, of British Midland Airways, was about to make an approach into Manchester when its right-outer engine (No.4) failed, the right inner (No.3) losing power moments later. Captain Harry Marlow initiated a right-hand orbit, his losing struggle being reflected in the Air Traffic log:

ATC: 'Go around, at 2,000 feet: what is your height?'
Aircraft: 'One thousand feet.'
ATC: 'Say again?'
Aircraft: '800 feet, and falling.'
ATC 'You have gone off the radar screen. – Hotel Golf? Hotel Golf?'

Forced to set the machine down, Captain Marlow selected the only undeveloped area he could see, the flight deck finishing up in a garage forecourt; the cabin on an electricity substation, where it burst into flames; and the tail on the bank of a ravine. Even then, rescuers found that many who had survived the impact had died in the fire, their legs trapped by the collapse of their seats.

It transpired that by a peculiarity in the Argonaut's fuel-system an engine could be starved of fuel. Further, that short-statured pilots were unable to reach the remedying control. It also emerged that at least three other operators were aware of the problem. Accordingly, Sir Elwyn Jones, QC, the Attorney General, found that shortcomings in design were the main cause. A finding which completely exonerated both the crew and British Midland, and led to dissemination of known hazards becoming an aviation-industry requirement.

VISITING THE SITE

In June 2002 a memorial to those who died was raised at the site, the junction of Waterloo Road and Hopes Carr, to be supplemented later, by one to the rescuers. At the second unveiling, Captain Marlow's sons received a bravery award on his behalf: trapped in the burning aircraft, their father's sole concern, continuously expressed, having been, 'How many passengers got out?'

The Waterloo Road, Hopes Carr memorial site

The plaque to those on board
'In memory of the seventy two passengers and crew who lost their
lives in the Stockport Air Disaster 4th June 1967'

The plaque to the rescuers: … (who) did not turn away.
'This memorial is dedicated to those involved in the rescue and who
gave aid at the Stockport Air Disaster 4th June 1967. All were faced
with the true horror of tragedy and did not turn away. Their courage
saved twelve lives.'

Chapel-en-le-Frith

14. Handley Page Hampden Mk.1 L4189
Black Edge, Dove Holes (north of Buxton)

SK 06389 76843 468 m

Unit and Station: No. 106 Squadron, RAF Finningley (Doncaster), No. 5 Group, Bomber Command

Date: 30 September 1940

Crew: four, three killed, one survived, injured

- Sergeant John Gray Gow, pilot
- Sergeant Charles Owen Cook, observer (navigator)
- Sergeant Eric Burt, wireless operator/air gunner
- Sergeant N. Powell, air gunner, injured

When Sergeant Pilot John Gow's trainee crew were detailed to fly a night navigational exercise on 30 September 1940, they were approaching the end of their operational training. It is not known how experienced Sergeant Charles Cook was as a navigator – the aircrew category 'Observer' was to be re-designated 'Navigator' in 1942 – but Sergeant Pilot Gow had logged just 200 hours, forty of which were on the Hampden. As the sortie was designed to give a foretaste of operational conditions, radio silence was imposed. There came time, however, due, in part to the cloudy conditions obtaining, when the crew were forced to admit to being totally lost.

There was no danger, provided they maintained a safe altitude, and they feared that calling for navigational assistance might delay their being cleared as fit for operations. Having tried all they knew, however, both pilot and navigator submitted resolutely, directing the wireless operator to call Finningley for a course to steer. (In the parlance of the morse brevity code, *'QDM IMI'* – 'What is my magnetic course to steer for your station?') In those days, however, the procedure took a considerable time, for the aircraft then had to transmit two ten-second dashes, separated by its callsign. Even so, within thirty seconds or so, the Finningley direction-finder was able to send the sanctuary-affording course-to-steer.

Tragically, before an acknowledgement could be tapped out, let alone in time for Sergeant Gow to respond and turn onto the given heading, contact was lost, the Hampden having crashed into Black Edge, where it had exploded and burst into flames. The inquiry had to assume that, in trying to determine their position, the crew had begun a blind descent through cloud, for they struck at just 1,530 feet.

As might be expected, having impacted at some 217 mph (189 knots) there was no hope for the three crew stationed forwards, but incredibly the gunner, Sergeant Powell, survived the crash, seriously injured though he was. Indeed, he was doubly fortunate, for although the cloud had masked the aircraft's navigation lights, the sound of the crash enabled local farmers to reach the scene in time to drag him clear of the flames.

Mr Bill Hollinrake, who had been working at Blackedge Farm, recalled, 'The plane had crashed in what we call Coltsfield, the gunner being brought down through the Hundred Acres field to the road.'

Mr John Prince, of Brookhouse Farm, even secured a parachute, intending to have his wife make handkerchiefs. When no handkerchiefs appeared, however, there were those who held that the lady had found a more intimate use for the silk.

VISITING THE SITE

Black Edge is a fine ridge which well repays the climb. Lay-by parking is available beside the A6 at SK 07483 77261, but the off-path ascent requires a railway crossing. The sensible option is to seek courtesy parking near Blackedge Farm then follow the farm's track to SK 07045 76481 (1,148 feet, 350 m) before climbing off-path for the final 800 yards (and 400-plus vertical feet). In late 2013 only a few globs of molten metal remained.

*The Black Edge impact site, looking towards Thorn Head Farm,
late 2013*

Detail of the debris pool

15. FZG76 V1 (*Vergeltungswaffe 1*) Fieseler Fi103) Flying Bomb
Hob Tor, Black Edge, Dove Holes (north of Buxton)

SK 06178 77911 471 m
Luftwaffe: air-launched by Heinkel He111s of No. 53 *Kampfgeschwader*
(KG53: No. 53 Bomber Group)
Date: 24 December 1944

Although the major air-launched attack of Flying Bombs on the Midlands, some fifty of them, occurred on Christmas Eve 1944, local remembrances insist that some fell as early as the June of that year. One of those in this disputed category is the V1 which exploded on Black Edge, south of Chapel-en-le-Frith, which officially-derived sources record as having landed at 0545 hours during the Christmas-Eve attack.

Among several residents who remembered the incident, Mrs Henrietta Craven, of Rye Flatt Farm, Combs, was adamant that, 'It was certainly not on Christmas Eve.'

And Mr and Mrs Bill and Jean Hollinrake, of Peak Forest, had especial cause to remember the date, 'At the time,' Mr Hollinrake recalled, 'I was labouring at Blackedge Farm, below Black Edge, and earlier that night we'd been out to celebrate our engagement. So it wasn't Christmas Eve ...'

Indeed, it was their son, Mr Stephen Hollinrake, who was able to re-identify the site. 'In the sixties,' he remembered, 'I'd struck out from the ridge and was following the minor path past the crater, when I came upon a section of jet pipe, and threw it back into the water.'

VISITING THE SITE

It is likely that this site will be visited in association with the nearby Hampden site (see above). The crater, being shallow, is singularly different from the myriad disused mining pits along the Edge, the peat having dissipated the effects of the ton or so of amatol high explosive.

*V1 Flying Bomb crater, Hob Tor, early 2013. In more typical weather,
a sludge-filled pool*

Flying Bomb crater, Hob Tor, its more normal aspect

Buxton area

16. Noorduyn Norseman UC-64A 43-35439
Shining Tor, west of Buxton

SJ 99830 73579 517 m
Unit and Station: United States Ninth Army Air Force,
Allied Expeditionary Force, 10th Air Depot Group,
10th Air Depot Repair Squadron, RAF Burtonwood
Date: 29 September 1944
Crew: pilot, slightly injured
• Second Lieutenant Arnold Fredrickson, USAAF

On 29 September 1944 Second Lieutenant Arnold Fredrickson, a United States Army Air Force ferry pilot, was returning to RAF Burtonwood (just east of Liverpool), from a delivery flight to RAF Winthrop, near Newark, Nottinghamshire. Having encountered, as he later recorded, 'Just five minutes cloud', on his forty-five minute inbound flight, he filed a ground-contact clearance for the return. As it was, the weather had changed considerably, with low cloud over the hills, showers reducing visibility below, and a freshened headwind to slow his groundspeed by 30 knots. Though with less than five hundred hours' flying experience, Second Lieutenant Fredrickson, unlike so many pilots of his era, did, at least, elect to climb to a safe altitude to carry out the flight. And when he found himself bucking, as his accident report reflects, 'fog and a terrific headwind', he reasoned that adding an hour to his estimates would see him clear of the high ground.

Accordingly, when the time was up, and confident that he was now over the low-lying Cheshire Plain, he commenced his descent through the cloud. By 2,300 feet on his altimeter he was settled onto his instruments, but as he reached 1,800 feet he glimpsed hills immediately ahead, and hastily powering up, adopted a climbing attitude – only to impact with the ground.

The aircraft turned over and, with virtually full tanks, burnt fiercely. But Second Lieutenant Fredrickson, barely injured, resolutely kicked himself clear. He initially found succour at Stake Farm, after which he was taken to the Cat and Fiddle Inn to await an ambulance.

The American Accident Committee found benignly that, 'The accident is solely a result of weather'. A benign finding Second Lieutenant Fredrickson must surely have reckoned as the second time Fortune had favoured him that day!

The Norseman crash site, below Shining Tor

For some years, until June 2010, this site had been associated with the Defiant which crashed nearby in October 1941. But then a heat-discharged cartridge case from a personal side arm, tellingly manufactured in 1942! was unearthed by researcher Professor Sean Moran's hiking pole.

Cartridge case from a 0.45 inch calibre Colt automatic personal side arm, manufactured in 1942, and exploded by heat

VISITING THE SITE

There is parking opposite the Cat and Fiddle Inn, and rather less where Errwood track leaves the A543 (SK 00006 72126, 500 m). After 0.72 miles – some 20 minutes – along the Errwood track, turning left onto the Shining Tor track for 580 yards to SJ 99689 73524, 530 m (where ruined field wall and path-side wall meet), positions the walker 155 yards from the crash site. This lies on 057°M into the moor over heather and bilberry. But, though rough and pathless, remember, this is what well-heeled shooters pay to walk over! In 2013 the burn scar (at that time fifty feet beyond shooting butt No.5), was still peppered with small debris.

A Harvard crash site (see next below) is then 200 yards distant on 339°M. From which Shining Tor, with its must-linger-at viewpoint (not forgetting the ridge path, with an end to heather and bilberry!), is 300 yards directly upslope on 270°M.

17. North American Harvard Mk.2B FT442
Shining Tor, near the Cat and Fiddle Inn, Buxton

SJ 99753 73746 530 m
Unit and Station: No. 5 (Pilots) Advanced Flying Unit, RAF Ternhill
(Market Drayton, Shropshire), No. 21 Group, Flying Training Command
Date: 30 November 1944
Crew: pilot, killed
- Sergeant Julius Sofranko, Czechoslovakian, in the Royal Air Force

Sergeant Julius Sofranko, a Czechoslovakian airman who had made his way
via Poland to the French *Armée de l'Air*, and so to the Royal Air Force, was
relatively experienced with over 300 hours total and 146 hours solo on type.
On 30 November 1944 he was flying on a solo navigational cross-country
when, two-and-a-half hours into the sortie, on the return leg to his RAF
Ternhill, Shropshire, base, he entered cloud and flew into the Shining Tor
ridge. He was killed, and the aircraft destroyed.

Harvard FT442 below Shining Tor

With the crash site being just thirty-six miles from Ternhill, the court of
inquiry was able to deduce that Sergeant Sofranko had commenced his
descent to base on an un-amended estimated-time-of-arrival, believing that
he was clear of high ground. It had been Sergeant Sofranko's misfortune that

since he had got airborne the wind had changed, so substantially reducing his speed over the ground that high terrain was still ahead of him when he blindly nosed down.

Shepherd Albert Heathcote who discovered the Harvard

Shepherd Mr Albert Heathcote, whose beat covered the whole ridge, was the first person to come across the Harvard. He craned to the badly shattered cockpit to see if he could help, only to realise that the pilot was beyond aid. Youthful Mr Heathcote was so horrified that he could never remember arriving home, although the alarm was duly raised. 'I gave the site a wide berth until it was cleared,' he recalled.

The contemporary photograph of the Harvard, on misty, apparently near-level ground, has raised doubts that the site given here is the terminal impact site, but, in fact, the slope is relatively shallow. Then again, the site matches that recorded by ranger Phil Shaw, when working with author Ron Collier, in 1970. The hollow originated with an amateurish attempt to salvage the valuable phosphor-bronze of the cylinder heads using explosives.

The demolition crater, below the impact site

Debris from the crater

VISITING THE SITE

The details given for visiting the Norseman site (see above), hold for this one, which lies a further 200 yards on, to the north-west (339°M). Shining Tor is then another 300 yards directly upslope on 270°M. By 2014 there was little to be seen, although poking around unearthed both metal and perspex.

18. Airspeed Oxford Mk.1 LX745
The Tors, northern slope of Shining Tor

SJ 99813 74626 500 m impact point
SJ 99818 74648 489 m embedded fuel tank
Unit and Station: No. 11 (Pilots) Advanced Flying Unit, RAF Calveley (north-west of Crewe), No. 21 group, Flying Training Command
Date: 12 March 1944
Crew: three, injured, then died of exposure
- Flying Officer Charles Stuart Grant Wood, pilot, instructor
- Pilot Officer Gerald Campbell Liggett, pilot under training
- Flight Sergeant Joseph George Hall, navigator/wireless operator

On 12 March 1944 staff instructor Flying Officer Charles Wood was tasked to supervise a trainee pilot on a night, radio-navigation cross-country. During the flight the navigating was to be done by Flight Sergeant Joseph Hall. However, as he was one of the unit's staff navigator/wireless operators, he was also expected to provide the various radio fixes, bearings, and weather updates.

A search was instituted once the aircraft became overdue, but not until a considerable time later was it found, shattered on the high moorland edge of Shining Tor, far to the south of the planned track, unburnt, but with the bodies of its crew huddled together alongside the major portion of the wreckage.

Furnished with the aircraft's radio-navigation log, the investigators were struck by the sparsity of entries. In particular they saw that the warning of a significant wind change had been missed. Further delving then showed that Flight Sergeant Hall had spent most of his post-qualifying time navigating rather than keeping his morse code up to scratch and operating the radio set.

The lack of radio-derived navigational information helped explain why captain and navigator had not only allowed trainee Pilot Officer Liggett to turn for base on the planned estimate, but to commence his descent, for at that time the aircraft was a full twenty-eight miles from Calveley, and still over high ground.

The investigators made various recommendations, but especially that the unit's dual-category aircrew – whether navigator/wireless operators or wireless operator/air gunners – should periodically demonstrate their continued efficiency as wireless operators. An understandable requirement, for while fulfilling the navigator's or gunner's role it was only too easy to lose the finesse demanded by the wireless equipment.

The investigators' terms of reference also obliged them to observe that Flying Officer Wood had not made use of the 'Darky' emergency 'get-you-down' facility. But, as aircrew themselves, they would have taken this as proof that nobody on board ever dreamt that they were in need of navigational assistance.

It is noteworthy too, that when the junior-officer investigators submitted that poor instrument flying was not a factor in this accident they were chastised by the Air Officer Commanding. Yet his ire is to be wondered at considering that the aircraft had been in a stable and perfectly-controlled descent when it struck, albeit undeniably out of position.

A fatally-ironic turn of events not recorded in the summary report of the crash investigation but verified by Mr Albert Heathcote, then shepherd of the Pym Chair-Shining Tor Ridge, is that the crew members, injured though they were, might well have made their way to safety. Except that, being either shocked, or intent on obeying the air-search precept that it is always best to stay with the aircraft – a downed machine being easier to see than a person –, they remained where they were, and not being found in time, died of exposure.

Impact site of Oxford LX745. The walkers include, centre, former veteran ranger and mountain-rescue-team-member Phil Shaw: his customary bare feet hidden by heather!

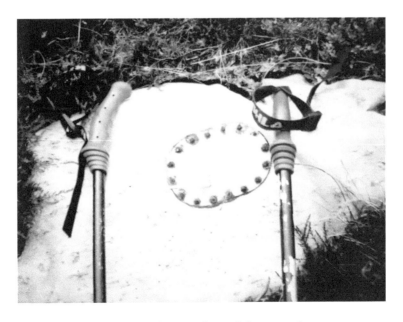

Detail of secondary debris pool

VISITING THE SITE

The crash site is rather closer to the parking at Pym Chair than to that near the Cat and Fiddle, though the splendid ridge path gives mustn't-miss panoramic views from either direction. A path, still vestigial in early 2014, branches off at SJ 99753 74656 (twixt Cats Tor and Shining Tor), the crash site bearing 094°M and only 200 feet from the junction, but concealed by very broken, heather-covered terrain. Probably the reason why so much debris remains, a central pool, and just feet away, an embedded fuel tank.

19. Republic P-47D Thunderbolts 42-7872 and 42-7898
Cats Tor, Shining Tor Ridge

SJ 99506 75402 480 m
Unit and Station: USAAF, 8th Fighter Command,
2906th Observation Group, Training HQ & HQ Squadron,
AAF342 (RAF Atcham), south-east of Shrewsbury
Date: 30 September 1943
Occupants: pilots, two, both killed
- Captain Malta L. Stepp Jnr, United States Army Air Force
- Staff Sergeant Lynn R. Morrison, USAAF

Steady attrition among the operational squadrons of the USAAF led to a constant need for replacement pilots. It was imperative, however, that these were introduced to the European environment. Accordingly, on getting airborne from RAF Atcham on a formation exercise, Staff Sergeant Lynn Morrison was led by Captain Malta Stepp Jr. who had two years' experience in the theatre, having served as a volunteer with the predominantly American No. 121 (Eagle) Squadron, RAF, only transferring to the USAAF in September 1942 when the Eagle squadrons were disbanded.

The weather was not that promising, with a general cloud base of just 1,500 feet. The visibility below the base, though, was given as unlimited so Captain Stepp headed north-eastwards, deciding that the terrain-delineated, below-cloud arena would afford adequate room for lateral manoeuvres, at least. These would have meant having Staff Sergeant Morrison fly in the various positions expected of a number two, easing smartly from one to the other, his attention focussed upon his leader except when periodically directed to open out to receive an updated position and to check his gauges.

And when, just twenty minutes after take off, he was led directly into the face of Cats Tor he was in a precise echelon-port position, impacting just feet upslope from his leader, dying, almost certainly without having even glimpsed the cloud-mantled ground, his last impression, perhaps, vague wonder that his leader should have so suddenly checked, then so disconcertingly flicked back past his right wing tip.

Though the tops were in cloud, a farmer heard the double impact and quickly raised the alarm. The accident investigators, however, for all their deliberations, were never able to find a rational explanation for Captain Stepp's having entered cloud when the hills he had been manoeuvring below rose a full three hundred feet higher than where he impacted.

They did speculate that something might have been wrong with Captain Stepp's radio, but only because no fix had been asked for. But then, only twenty minutes into the sortie, and flying in good visibility below the cloud, why would Captain Stepp have had need of one? After all, had he done, and doubted his own radio, he only had to get his number two to open out and make the call.

Self in the leader's impact crater, rucksack at the No.2's crater

Centre, a 0.5 inch calibre cartridge case found in the leader's crater

VISITING THE SITE

Closest parking is at SJ 99447 76797, with lay-by parking even closer to Pym Chair. The Shining Tor Ridge is enough to draw any walker, forget aircraft crash sites! However, this one is accessed by leaving the track – wiv scrupulous care for the fencing! – near the bottom of Cats Tor at SJ 99608 75410 (490 m). Having followed the drystone wall downslope for 240 feet the leader's impact site is to the right, forty feet off. By late 2013 it had become rare to find metal visually, while both 'craters' were duplicated, within feet, by natural patches of exposed peat.

20. De Havilland DH10 Amiens F357
(see also DH60X G-EBWA, next below)
Burbage Edge, Derbyshire Bridge

SK 02354 71587 463 m

Organisation: National Aircraft Factory No. 2, Heaton Chapel, Stockport, de Havilland assembly line, flown from Ringway,

on delivery to the Royal Air Force

Date: 8 December 1919

Crew: possibly three, but not known

Alan Jones' painting of DH10 F357 over Burbage Edge

On 8 December 1919 the factory pilot delivering DH10 F357 to the RAF got as far as Burbage Edge, ran into bad visibility, and crashed into the hillside.

Although researcher Ron Collier recorded this incident – so inspiring the painting by Alan Jones – datings vary, both the 18th and 24th of February 1919 having been put forward. Then again, in 2004, when being proprietorially shown the location was a matter of reverential tones and an air-crash anorak blood oath, it was intimated that another coven had taken away everything but some flecks of doped canvas beneath a rock.

Fortunately, Mr Bernard Minshull, of Goslin Bar Farm, Burbage, was able to independently supply the location, 'Only,' he warned, 'there's nothing now, just bits of canvas.' He went on, 'The Burbage Edge head keeper, Tom Bell, at Tunnel Farm, took the wheels to make a hand-cum-horse haycart. He and my Dad used it long before the war ...' He paused. 'According to Dad, mechanics from Park Garage – Hodgkinson's place in Buxton –, took the Sopwith's [sic] engines ...' In late 2010, however, although the garage owner had heard of the component he could not remember seeing it.

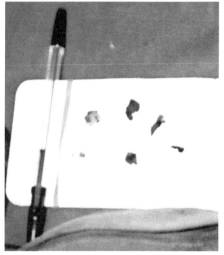

The crash site in mid 2013

Only flecks of doped canvas

VISITING THE SITE.

Parking can be found at Derbyshire Bridge, at SK 01860 71589, after which taking the Macclesfield Old Road to SK 02208 71756 leaves an off-path uphill trudge of some 240 yards. An alternative access route is that given for DH60 G-EBWA (see next below).

21. De Havilland DH60X Cirrus Moth G-EBWA
(see also DH10 F357 next above)
Burbage Edge, Derbyshire Bridge

DH60 Cirrus Moth

SK 02354 71587 463 m (provisional, see below)

Organisation: Herts and Essex Aeroplane Club, Nazeing, Essex

Date: 11 October 1934

Occupants: two, both slightly injured

- Mr William James Alington, pilot and owner
- Mr H. Ellis, passenger

Mr Alington's intended destination was Belfast, but while staging between Broxbourne (Essex) and Stanley Park (Blackpool) he ran into low cloud in extremely gusty conditions. Having experienced difficulty in maintaining control, he then became lost, and decided to make a precautionary landing. While positioning to do so, however, a particularly violent gust swept the Moth into Burbage Edge. Having cut themselves free, the occupants found they had only minor injuries, but the machine was in a sorry state; as Mr Alington, an RAF reservist, told a *Buxton Herald* reporter, 'the instrument panel … is in the passenger's seat, the machine is on its back, and its pieces are spread over the moor.'

As it was, after the outbreak of war, Mr Alington was again to find himself inverted in a crashed aircraft, this time, a Miles Master. But this was merely peripheral to a fine wartime career. Having flown nearly three thousand instructional hours by 1941, he was awarded the Air Force Cross. He then escaped from Flying Training Command and joined No. 25 Squadron to fly Ranger patrols in Mosquitoes, adding a Distinguished Flying Cross to his AFC. He eventually retired as a substantive wing commander.

This accident to G-EBWA appears as, the Ministry affirmed in early 2010, 'a one-liner on the non-investigated civil list as having occurred "Near Buxton". Recently, however, a section of panel, said to be from a Moth, and purporting to have been removed from the location given here, and then squirreled away, has appeared on anorak websites.

It seems then, that future researchers must find one of these venerable machines – the Moth or the Amiens – a new resting place.

VISITING THE SITE:

A convenient approach is to park in the A537 lay-by at SK 02800 71350, then follow Burbage Edge for a quarter of a mile northwards until abeam the location, descending then to the site. For an alternative route, see DH10 F357 above.

22. Airspeed Oxford Mk.1 EB717
Burbage Edge, east of Derbyshire Bridge

SK 02559 71720 495 m

Unit and Station: No. 11 (Pilots) Advanced Flying Unit,
RAF Calveley, near Crewe, No. 21 Group, Flying Training Command
Date: 2 May 1943
Crew: pupil pilot, killed

* Sergeant John Henry Langley Wilson

Sergeant John Wilson was relatively experienced for the day, with 280 hours total flying and 102 hours on Oxfords, both unusually high totals for a pupil. Just the same, in terms of general air-awareness his experience level was low, and when, in the course of a night cross-country from RAF Calveley, the weather deteriorated, he became, at best, uncertain of his position.

In the pre-dawn light, finding himself over a blacked-out but singularly-shaped town, he set up a wide circle, passing in and out of cloud as he tried to determine which town it was. Doing so would have meant his flying with one eye on the ground over the town side of his cockpit, and one on the map, as he tried to correlate the two.

His abstraction, however, evidently took his mind from his height keeping and the mist-obscured high ground over his shoulder, so much so that the Oxford gradually descended towards Burbage Edge, eventually breasting through a drystone wall and then disintegrating. Sergeant Wilson did not survive the impact.

With Buxton being so far off Sergeant Wilson's assigned routings, the court of inquiry looked into the possibility that some compass error had occurred. But they noted too that he had not called for radio assistance. Accordingly, they found for overconfidence.

The impact site of Oxford EB717

Debris from the rush-fringed hole

VISITING THE SITE

Having parked at Derbyshire Bridge (SK 01860 71589), taking the Macclesfield Old Road for 700 yards to SK 02328 71900 leaves the site 300 yards uphill and to the right (173°M). There is no path, but the going is not too bad. The only visual evidence at the scene, however, is the broken wall the Oxford ploughed through, in which recently detected metal might have been left, together with an arm-deep, reed-fringed pool which has for long contained both metal and plywood skinning.

23. FZG76 V1 (Vergeltungswaffe 1) Fieseler Fi103) Flying Bomb Tunnel Farm, Burbage, Buxton

SK 02998 73723 448 m

Luftwaffe: Air-launched by Heinkel He111s of No. 53 *Kampfgeschwader* (KG53: No. 53 Bomber Group)

Date: 24 December 1944

The ramp-launched V1 pulse-jet Flying Bomb had a range of only a hundred miles or so, however, as the Allies began imperilling the launching sites, V1s were mounted below Heinkel One-Eleven bombers and air-launched from the North Sea. The major – and final – attack came on Christmas Eve 1944 when some fifty were dispatched, one of them falling on farmland bordering the open moorland of Burbage Edge, above Tunnel Farm, Burbage.

As one resident remembered, 'The whole sky seemed to be lit up by the flare from the Doodlebug's back end,' while another recalled how the then incumbent of Tunnel Farm, Keeper Mr Tom Bell, would maintain that only the slope of the hill saved him, that even then, the blast blew his hat off.'

Crater above Tunnel Farm

VISITING THE SITE

Opportunity parking might be found anywhere beyond Bishop's Lane, after which the dismantled railbed towards Tunnel Farm will allow an off-path ascent to Burbage Edge. In truth, the crater referenced here relies upon little more than a similarity to proven V1 craters. However, Mr Bernard Minshull, of Goslin Bar Farm, described the general impact area above Tunnel Farm, 'On the downslope, but short of the Burbage Edge wall and the moor proper.'

24. Airspeed Oxford Mk.1 HN429
Axe Edge, south of Buxton

SK 03156 69217 544 m

Unit and Station: No. 11 (Pilots) Advanced Flying Unit, RAF Calveley, north-west of Crewe, No. 21 Group, Flying Training Command

Date: 3 November 1944

Crew: three, all injured

- Flying Officer C.V. Mayhead, RAF Volunteer Reserve, staff instructor, pilot
- Flying Officer A.C. Mullen, Royal Canadian Air Force, pupil pilot
- Flying Officer J.S. Bean, Royal Canadian Air Force, pupil pilot

On 3 November 1944 Flying Officer Mayhead, an Advanced Flying Unit staff instructor, was tutoring two pupil pilots in Standard Beam Approach (SBA) techniques. Although effectively the forerunner of all modern bad-weather landing systems, SBA demanded a lot more from crews, and in its earliest form required constant monitoring of headphone signals. Significantly, in order to talk to ground control, or even to use the intercom, the pilot might have to temporarily switch away from – and so lose – some vital SBA signals.

The initial step was to home the aircraft to the airfield, so fixing its position. The aircraft would then be flown away from the airfield and down the beam for three miles to an 'outer marker' beacon. After that, a fixed-pattern 'procedure turn' would leave it facing the airfield. At which point, knowing that he was within five miles of the field and, therefore, in a zone guaranteed clear of high ground, the pilot would begin his approach. Straightforward enough in the classroom, but in the air it could be very confusing.

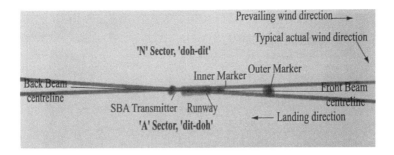

SBA diagram

Evidently, on this occasion, the operating pupil-pilot of Oxford HN429 found it so, for in flying outbound he lost the beam. And compounding that, in attempting to steer back onto it, he turned the wrong way. Which meant that at 163 mph he was diverging further from the centre-line every second. So it was that, although he maintained 1,650 feet on his altimeter – and quite likely just as instructor Flying Officer Mayhead decided it was time to take a hand – the aircraft flew into the shoulder of 1,800 foot Axe Edge, sixteen miles off the centre-line. The Oxford was totally destroyed, but there was no fire, and though injured, the crew survived.

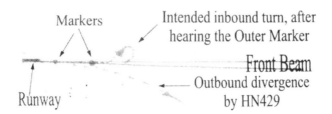

Divergent track from SBA beam

The court of inquiry found that the operating pilot had failed to adapt quickly enough to the technique required for tracking the beam outbound. It found too that, flying in cloud, he had underestimated the wind effect helping to drift him off the beam. Additionally, that in switching from radio to intercom he had missed the vital outer-marker signal. The accident, however, was recognised as one inherent in beam training, so no disciplinary action resulted. As a positive result, though, the heights for the positioning procedure at Calveley were raised.

Impact site of Oxford HN429

VISITING THE SITE

There is lay-by parking on the A53 at SK 02777 71368 (490 m). The ridge path, vestigial but airily pleasing – the sprawl of Buxton's laboratory complex excepted –, can most sedately be picked up by threading a stile at SK 03398 69779 then zig-zagging upslope. After some 700 yards (twenty minutes), at SK 03232 69199, the site lies 250 feet downslope on 283°M. In late 2013 a moderate pool of debris remained, in a hollow, amid the bilberry and cotton grass.

25. Douglas A-20G Havoc (Boston) 43-9958
Quarnford (near Flash), A53, Buxton-Leek road

SK 03212 68074 448 m

Unit and Station: Eighth USAAF, 310th Ferry Squadron, 27th Air Transport Group, AAF169 (RAF Stanstead)

Date: 3 January 1945

Crew: pilot, killed

* First Lieutenant Eugene H. Howard, United States Army Air Force (USAAF)

On 3 January 1945 First Lieutenant Eugene Howard was ferrying Havoc 43-9958 as one of a batch from Stanstead to be delivered to the USAAF's Base Air Depot at Burtonwood, near Liverpool.

The en-route weather featured cloud on the hills with low visibility in rain, in view of which a left turn was planned at Leicester which would temporarily head the Havocs towards Chester and so, keep them clear of high ground. Significantly, however, there was also a 35 knot wind from the left at cruising altitude. And 'significantly' because, while all the other pilots arrived safely, First Lieutenant Howard strayed twenty-one miles right of track and was killed when he struck high ground an hour after take off at Quarnford, near Flash.

What caused First Lieutenant Howard to stray so far off track could not be positively established, but it seems likely that he failed to compensate for the strong wind from his left. It is equally possible, though, that he turned right at Leicester instead of left. For although he had logged 1,200 hours' flying overall this was his first ever flight on the Havoc. As it was, he commenced a let-down through cloud, clearly believing himself to be over the Chester Plain when, in fact, he was descending into southern outliers of Axe Edge.

The accident committee had to record his descent through cloud as an error of judgement. But they did allow his total unfamiliarity with the Havoc to stand as a possible contributory factor.

The Havoc impact site

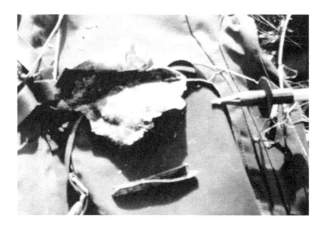

Havoc debris

VISITING THE SITE

Opportunity parking can be found by the A53 at SK 03120 67941 (on the map, see New Lodge Farm). The site lies 170 yards off on 030°M along the line of a drystone wall. Debris shards can be found, but this seems subject to farming activity.

26. FZG76 V1 (*Vergeltungswaffe 1*) Fieseler Fi103) Flying Bomb
Clough House Farm, Langley, Macclesfield Forest

SJ 95501 72672 276 m

Luftwaffe: Air-launched by Heinkel He111s of No. 53 *Kampfgeschwader*
(53KG: No. 53 Bomber Group)

Date: 24 December 1944

One of the fifty pilotless, V1 pulse-jet flying bombs air-launched on 24
December 1944 landed at Langley, at Clough House Farm. The Cantrell
family, their attention attracted by a stuttering engine sound, saw a
machine, and then flames, and initially thought it was an aircraft in trouble.
An abrupt cessation to the engine noise, however, soon disabused them.
A few moments of breathless anticipation followed. Then came a massive
explosion.

Making their way to the nearby, suddenly roofless, Crooked Yard Farm,
it was to find the incumbent, Mrs Frances Barnes, mortified at being seen,
for having been kneeling to light the fire when the V1 landed, soot had
covered her from head to toe.

Mr John Cantrell was able to show the still impressive crater. 'Until the
seventies,' he remembered, 'there was a metal tube around the place – the
jet pipe. But it's long gone.'

John Cantrell in the Clough House Farm crater

VISITING THE SITE

A footpath branching from the rewarding Pegg's Nose area runs just south of Clough House Farm and at SJ 95619 72510 crosses a track. The crater is 220 yards down this (on 327°M), to the north-east (the right) of the fence. Alternatively, parking might be begged at the private Clough House Farm (descending the very narrow road from Walker Barn, on the A537).

27. De Havilland Vampire FB Mk.5 VV602
Torgate Farm, Wildboarclough, west of the Cat and Fiddle Inn

SJ 98612 71930 306 m crater
SJ 98443 71980 384 m pilot
Unit and Squadron: No. 613 Royal Auxiliary Air Force Squadron, Ringway (Manchester), No. 12 Group, Fighter Command
Date: 1 May 1954
Crew: pilot, killed, unsuccessful manual bale out
• Flying Officer Jocelyn Francis Baverstock Davis, Royal Auxiliary Air Force

On 1 May 1954, when two Royal Auxiliary Air Force Vampire FB – fighter-bomber – Mk.5s took off to carry out a cinema-gun combat practice at a briefed, 'above 25,000 feet', Flying Officer Jocelyn Davis was to fly as the Number Two. A South African who, in his day job, worked for the Metropolitan Vickers Electrical Company, he had not long been married.

The sky was thundery, and as the pair climbed through 6,000 feet, now in thick cloud, Flying Officer Davis, losing station, made the advisory call, 'Breaking', following this with an unclear transmission, after which nothing more was heard from him.

Mr John Bowler, of Torgate Farm, witnessed the outcome. 'The plane dived almost vertically into the ground and exploded,' he said. 'There was a parachute, but it stayed with the plane for some time, then came free. Only it never opened properly.' He paused. 'I ran to the phone at the Stanley Arms – a nearby farm-cum-pub – while Eileen, my sister, went to the plane.' He paused. 'And, half-way down the hill came across the pilot's body ...'

It was clear to the inquiry that, having lost control, Flying Officer Davis had wisely decided to bale out. Only, unaccountably, his parachute had opened in the cockpit! subsequently snagging, and ripping. Just the same, medical evidence established that he had actually been killed by striking the high-set tailplane, an only too-well-known pre-ejection-seat occurrence on the Vampire.

The findings blamed Flying Officer Davis's inexperience in instrument flying, recommending, therefore, the provision of a dual Vampire to provide single-seater pilots with regular practise.

Mr Bowler recalled too, the pilot's widow being brought to the hillside some days later, her voice breaking as she murmured, 'At least he found a green field.'

The Vampire's engine was found 18 feet down, embedded in rock, and was left there. But debris was spread as far as the Cuckoo Rocks, half a mile away. Then again, so many shards were left that lime had to be spread to dissuade the cows from eating the yet hazard-laden grasses.

Mr John Bowler, where the pilot landed

The impact crater

Debris from the crater

VISITING THE SITE

There is limited parking off the Wildboarclough road at SJ 98178 71364. A north-easterly track then leads some 800 yards to the crater – now a grassy depression – which lies inside the boundary fence of the Broughsplace private holding.

Each of these sites has been proven by metal-detector search – most showing positive traces of aircraft material – while others have been identified by photographs and witness testimony, an example of each method being shown. Top illustration, below, shows an identifiable component, in this instance from a 1919 DH9A, now in a private collection. The lower illustration shows photographic evidence, illustrated by a Blenheim crash on Woolley Flats, Glossop. Page 111 evidences witness testimony, in this case erstwhile shepherd Tom Adlington at a Wellington crash site.

The brass petrol-tank cap of a DH9A, stamped for the Aeronautical Inspectorate Directorate

Blenheim K7172 inverted at Woolley Bridge, although buildings have altered, the landowner was able to re-identify the spot

Former shepherd, Mr Tom Adlington, at the crash site of Wellington Z8491, White Edge Moor

Buxton area

1. De Havilland DH85 Leopard Moth AV986
Rushup Edge summit

SK 11230 83450 540 m, Lord's Seat

Unit and Station: No. 14 Ferry-Pilots Pool, RAF Ringway (Manchester), Air Transport Auxiliary, RAF Maintenance Command

Date: 30 August 1941

Crew: pilot, uninjured

- First Officer Bernard Short, Air Transport Auxiliary

Flight Captain Bernard Short, Air Transport Auxiliary

On 30 August 1941 First Officer Bernard Short, an Air Transport Auxiliary pilot from the ferry pool at Ringway (Manchester), was tasked to deliver Leopard Moth AV986 to an anti-aircraft liaison unit. Having been airborne for just fifteen minutes, as he told the inquiry, his engine gave him so much concern that he made a precautionary landing on the high-level spine of Rushup Edge, near Lord's Seat, above Edale.

Evidently carrying out the repair did not take long, for within minutes, again according to his testimony, he was ready to depart once more. On the take-off run, however, a gust caused him to strike a drystone wall, breaking a wing off the machine and collapsing its undercarriage. First Officer Short sustained no injuries.

The Lord's Seat set-down area

The Moth was deemed repairable at depot, and having been dismantled, was transported to Ringway by road. First Officer Short received only mild censure from the RAF court of inquiry and resumed his ferrying duties.

Yet what an intriguing incident! And how similar to that on the Helvellyn summit ridge in Lakeland where, in 1926, an aviator achieved some degree of fame – or notoriety – by landing on the stony ridge! But that aviator successfully got airborne again. Again, why put down with a doubtful engine on a high ridge when a mere jiggle of the stick would permit a glide into a green vale with farms in plenty to supply aid? True, with some 1,100 hours' flying, and 300 on Moths, First Officer Short was considerably more experienced than most pilots of his era; always discounting that eleven hundred hours has long been recognised as one of those danger points at which the tyro pilot might exhibit signs of overconfidence. All very intriguing …

Be that as it may, on 24 January 1944, some two and a half years after his Rushup Edge misadventure – and having logged another thousand hours –, the promoted Flight Captain Bernard Shaw was tasked to ferry Halifax heavy-bomber JP182 from RAF Kinloss, near Inverness, 425 miles south to RAF Kemble, in Wiltshire. In descending blind through blizzard conditions to re-locate himself, however, he crashed into the summit of Eel Crag (Crag Hill), near Keswick, in the Lake District, he and his engineer, ATA Senior Flight Engineer Arthur Bird, dying instantly.

Cloud shrouded Eel Crag, showing the impact point

VISITING THE SITE

Little debris would have been left on Rushup Edge site, for the Moth did little more than subside, and any bits which fell off would been easily visible to the salvage crew. Certainly, several hours of assiduous metal-detecting along every wall, past and present, with the aim of positively determining the terminal impact site, produced nothing even remotely aircraft-related.

So let the walker, pausing at Lord's Mount, pick out any line where the family car could safely be accelerated up to 40 mph, as lifting off a Moth required. But what a stirring Edge to walk! And what views over the Hope Valley!

Halifax Mk.2 JP182, Lake District
NY 19303 20390 817 m impact point
NY 19563 20584 563 m sheepfold debris
NY 19548 20618 547 m debris in hollows

Impact area debris, Eel Crag

Debris pool below Eel Crag

2. Supermarine Spitfire Mk.2A P7883
Rushup Edge, Edale

SK 10854 83536 505 m impact point of aircraft

SK 10890 83455 520 m terminal point of aircraft

SK 10380 83745 424 m map, in hollow

SK 10356 83845 394 m mae west

SK 10561 84264 294 m pilot

SK 09284 82558 451 m debris dragged to road for disposal

Unit and Station: No. 53 Operational Training Unit (OTU), RAF Hibaldstow (near Brigg, Lincolnshire), No. 9 Group, Air Defence of Great Britain Command

Date: 10 December 1943

Crew: pilot, injured

- Sergeant Ronald A. Mitchell

Former Sergeant Ronald Mitchell, mid 1980s

On 10 December 1943, when an accident report was raised on Spitfire P7883, its parent unit, No. 53 OTU, was part of Air Defence of Great Britain Command. Not that its pilot, Sergeant Ronald Mitchell, was directly engaged in air-defence duties, for as an OTU pupil he was practising formation flying with three other Spitfires.

As the sortie progressed, deteriorating weather forced the leader to shift ever-further westwards. But periodically he would have – certainly *should* have – advised his followers of their whereabouts in case they got separated. What he did do on occasion was open them out to allow them to check their cockpits, for Sergeant Mitchell suddenly found that his fuel-gauge was indicating zero.

Understandably enough, he was rattled. For a start, he lost the formation, but then, having been given an easterly homing for base, he cruised off to the west! Although, rationalising this, he expected to be over coastal Lincolnshire, so to get a heading ostensibly sending him out to sea would have fought against every directional sense. As it was, he steered even deeper into Derbyshire's cloud-covered high ground.

Not long later, indeed, as his leader was still endeavouring to set up a rendezvous, Sergeant Mitchell saw a sudden darkening of the cloud, and only just managed to bring the nose up before flying into the ground.

There was no fire, but he was left with a broken leg, arm, and nose, on a high, remote moorland that was most certainly not Lincolnshire, and upon which a December blizzard had now closed with a vengeance.

Researcher Professor Sean Moran on the Spitfire impact point

Spitfire terminal point, following blizzard conditions ...

The air search was hampered by the weather, but also by not knowing whereabouts Sergeant Mitchell had gone down. Mr Ron Townsend, a former member of the Peak Climbing Club, remembered when the search was finally launched, twenty-four hours after the crash. 'Having planned a midnight walk on Kinder,' he recalled, 'we'd had a few preparatory drinks with Bill Heardman in the Church Hotel – it's The Ramblers' Inn now – when a police inspector alerted us. Apparently a wing had been seen on Rushup Edge.'

His party, he remembered, had been searching above the Chapel Gate path when they came upon a aircraft map in a hollow. At which stage they were joined by a team descending from Rushup Edge who had found the aircraft, but not the pilot.'

One of that team, Mr Jack Bricklebank, later an aspirant Naval pilot, described what they had found. 'He'd struck hard', he said, 'then pancaked on the top. So while the wings had broken off the fuselage was pretty well intact.'

Consulting, and having considered the various descent routes, they concluded that the pilot had taken the broad ridge sloping gently westwards.

Spitfire pilot's route down

Mae west found discarded, below the track

'We soon came across a yellow lifejacket,' resumed Mr Townsend, 'partially buried in snow. But it was bloodstained!'

Even so, a hopeful start. Except that by four in the morning they were forced to call off the search. They snatched a meal at Edale, and were preparing to set out again when they learnt that an official search party, now on the moor, had come across the pilot in a gully near the Cowburn Tunnel.

The court of inquiry, concluding that the fuel gauge had probably been faulty, put the major blame onto the weather.

It was six months before Sergeant Mitchell got back into the air. But when Ranger Peter Jackson met him in the 1980s, he joked about his flying history. 'Shortly after getting my wings I had a mid-air collision near Edinburgh, and crashed. After which I flew into Rushup Edge, and crashed again. And then, just a few days before VE Day, flying a Mustang over Germany, I was shot up by a – supposedly friendly – Russian fighter!'

Even so, former Sergeant Mitchell remained in the RAF until 1947, went on to first-generation jets, and – as he told Ranger Jackson – 'Had to be pulled kicking and screaming from the cockpit.'

In 1980, Mr Maurice Oaks, of Barber Booth, escorted researcher Mr John Ownsworth to the site and described how he had sledged the wreckage behind his tractor to a Queen Mary trailer on the Chapel-Castleton Road, observing, 'There wasn't much left anyway.'

When Mr Bricklebank heard this, however, he smiled. 'But Ben Twig, who found the Spitfire with me, took the altimeter.' His smile became pensive. 'Ben's long gone now, but he became one of the earliest members of the RAF Mountain Rescue Service.'

The point on the Chapel-Castleton Road to which the debris was dragged

VISITING THE SITE

The site is best reached from Mam Tor car park, turning from the main path beyond Lord's Seat at SK 10929 83340 when the terminal impact site bears 343°M, 125 yards off. Exhaustive metal-detecting, however, has proved fruitless. But any excuse to get walkers onto Rushup Edge!

3. Avro Tutor K3308
Mill Cottages, Edale

SK 13500 85183 252 m

Unit and Station: Station Flight, RAF Duxford (Cambridgeshire),

No. 12 Group, Fighter Command

Date: 7 May 1940

Crew: pilot, survived

- Sergeant I. Hutchinson, RAF Volunteer Reserve

On 7 May 1940 Sergeant Hutchinson, of Station Flight RAF Duxford, became lost and ran short of fuel while ferrying Tutor K3308 to No. 11 Maintenance Unit's Aircraft Storage facility at Kirkbride, near Dumfries. The RAF's accident investigation summary, the Form 1180, recorded in telegraphese what action Sergeant Hutchinson took: 'Landed in the only available space which was too small. Even with terrific sideslipping he could not get into field, ran aircraft deliberately into trees of river bank.' In fact, Sergeant Hutchinson had chosen the trees as an alternative to plunging into the deeply ravined River Noe.

As Sergeant Hutchinson had flown only two hours' solo on the Tutor, the incident was blamed on lack of experience and lack of care in map reading. Consequently he was given a Dutch-uncle homily from his flight commander, and further instruction in map reading and navigation.

Tutor set-down site, Edale Mill

VISITING THE SITE

The site can be visited from the Lower Hollings or Backtor Bridge tracks, depending upon the closest opportunity parking. There is, of course, no evidence of the mishandled precautionary landing, but the otherwise-hidden gorge-powered flow which formerly fed Edale Mill is well worth discovering.

Castleton

4. Klemm light aeroplane
Camphill Gliding Club, Great Hucklow

SK 17840 78833 407 m (area of)
Date: 30 August 1937
Crew: pilot, Fraülein Eva Schmidt, uninjured

Klemm

Camp Hill

In August 1937 Herr Wolf Hirth, a pioneer in soaring, and aerial launching and towing, made an English tour to promote the two-seater version of his Miminoa glider. Included in his party were Fraüleins Eva Schmidt and Hanna Reitsch, each a celebrated aviatrix in her own right. On visiting the Camphill Gliding Club at Great Hucklow during the British National Gliding Championships Fraülein Schmidt used a Klemm light aeroplane as transport, launcher, and aerial tug. On 30 August 1937, however, the day before the group were due to leave, Fraülein Schmitt, flying the Klemm, struck the remnants of a drystone wall. The German crew, assisted by the club engineer, repaired the damage and successfully got their machine away on time.

In 1954 Fraülein Hanna Reitsch very nearly made a return visit. In the interim she had proved the efficacy of barrage balloon cables by deliberately flying into them, and had test flown machines as diverse as pioneer helicopters, the rocket-powered Messerschmitt Me163, and the jet-propelled Messerschmitt Me262. She had been promoted to *Flugkapitan* (captain) and awarded the Iron Cross and Luftwaffe Diamond Clasp. However, having been an enthusiastic supporter of Hitler, she was refused a visa.

Hanna Reitsch

VISITING THE SITE

Camphill Farm later became the Hucklow Gliding Club, and the fragmented wall which upset both the Klemm and the Master (next below) has long since been removed. The view from the plateau, however, is well worth the climb.

5. Miles Master Mk.3 W8761
Camphill Farm, Great Hucklow

SK 17840 78833 407 m approximate terminal area
Unit and Station: No. 16 (Polish) Service Flying Training School,
RAF Newton, No. 21 Group, Flying Training Command
Date: 21 March 1943
Crew: two, pupil and instructor, unhurt,
Polish Air Force under British Command:
- Flight Lieutenant Edward Suszyński
- Sergeant Henryk Raczkowski

On 21 March 1943 instructor Flight Lieutenant Edward Suszyński was detailed to fly with pupil pilot Sergeant Henryk Raczkowski while leading two solo pupils in a formation exercise. An hour after leaving Newton, when the trio ran into cloudy, poor visibility conditions, the two formating aircraft lost the leader, at which Flight Lieutenant Edward Suszyński realised that he had also lost himself.

Thirty minutes later, sighting the Camphill Farm windsock through a gap, he dived down. Only to land long, strike a drystone wall, and tip the Master onto its nose. Meanwhile, the two solo pupils had successfully located Newton and landed safely. The damaged Master, though, had to be recovered by road.

Flight Lieutenant Suszyński was mildly censured but later flew operations on Blenheims and Mosquitoes. On 11 July 1944, however, he went missing, by which time he had been awarded the Silver Cross – the fifth grade of the *Virtuti Militari*, Poland's senior award for gallantry –, and the Cross for Valour. Sergeant Raczkowski became operational on Spitfires and Hurricanes and finished the war as a warrant officer.

Great Hucklow

VISITING THE SITE

See Klemm light aeroplane, above.

6. Airspeed Oxford Mk.1 DF485
Castleton, near Hope

SK 15773 83191 170 m

Unit and Station: No. 42 Operational Training Unit, RAF Ashbourne, No. 70 Group, Army Co-operation Command

Date: 19 February 1943

Crew: three, and one passenger, all uninjured

- Flying Officer W.M. Bray, Royal Canadian Air Force, pilot
- Two aircrew trainees, and one passenger, all unidentified

On 19 February 1943 Flying Officer Bray, an American serving with the Royal Canadian Air Force, took off from Ashbourne with his trainee crew on a cross-country exercise in Oxford DF485. After two hours, flying at 1,200 feet, often through rough weather, the navigator, head down over his charts became airsick and was unable to continue working. Half an hour later Flying Officer Bray called upon his wireless operator to get him a course to steer for Ashbourne. Being at such a low altitude, however, the wireless operator was unable to make contact. At that point the turbulence markedly increased and after a particularly severe wing drop, Flying Officer Bray lost control, the machine beginning to spiral.

He managed to make a partial recovery, but only at an estimated two hundred feet. Shaken, but finding a field directly in front of him, he dropped his flaps, and leaving his wheels up – in accordance with contemporary standard procedure –, hastily put the Oxford down, even then clipping a tree before settling.

Farmer Irvin Robinson ran to give what assistance he could. Only four days before a Wellington bomber had crashed catastrophically on the far side of his farm (see HF613, above). And now! But this machine bellied to a halt, the crew shakily emerging. On arriving, though, Mr Robinson was puzzled. 'But I could have sworn,' he told the pilot, 'there were four of you.'

The pilot pointed to a figure hurrying towards the Castleton Road.

'We'd a chap along for the ride,' he explained, 'not signed in, so we've packed him off before anyone asks questions.'

Questions were asked, of course, by the court of inquiry. But not that one. While the Air Officer Commanding concurred with the inquiry's recommendation that no further action need be taken. For there was nothing to censure. Nothing, for example, like carrying unauthorised persons aboard one of His Majesty's aircraft.

The terminal area of Oxford DF485

VISITING THE SITE

No trace remains of the incident, indeed, a filtering plant – long redundant by 2013 – was constructed over the touchdown point.

7. Percival Proctor Mk.3 HM324
Middle Hill, Wormhill Moor, Hargatewall

SK 10822 77052 353 m

Unit and Station: Metropolitan Communications Squadron,
RAF Northolt, No. 47 Group, Transport Command.

Date: 5 March 1945

Occupants: pilot and two passengers; two killed, one passenger mortally injured

1. Pilot Officer Raouil Eugene Clements Serruys, Royal Belgian Air Force
2. Two passengers: unidentified

On 5 March 1945 Pilot Officer Raouil Serruys, of the Royal Belgian Air Force, was detailed to carry two passengers on a flight that took him north-west into the Buxton area. The Midlands weather was poor, with low cloud and even lower visibility beneath it, conditions which must have been instrumental in causing Pilot Officer Serruys to fly into the crest of Middle Hill, on Wormhill Moor. The aircraft shed a north-westerly trail of debris, demolishing a drystone wall and coming to a stop just yards into the field beyond.

The weather was so bad that the machine was not located until the next day when it was found that one of the occupants had managed to crawl downhill into the field below the crash site, only to perish overnight.

Though it was clear that Pilot Officer Serruys had become lost, the court of inquiry deliberated over whether he had descended blind in order to pinpoint himself, or sought to make a precautionary landing as his fuel ran low. Finding that his fuel tanks, though ruptured, had been virtually empty, they decided upon the latter.

Pilot Officer Serruys was criticised for not returning to base on encountering bad weather, or for not putting down in good time at an airfield. On the other hand, describing him as a pilot 'with little experience' – although 500 hours seems reasonable for that era –, they declared that he should never have been dispatched in such weather: a direct slap in the face for the authorising officer!

Mr Teddy Mosely, of Knotlow Farm, Wormhill, saw the Proctor next day. 'Being orange-coloured it stood out well,' he remembered. 'It had finished up by the rough area on the summit and for many years we'd plough up pieces of aluminium, but I can't remember when any last surfaced.'

A metal-detector search discovered just two scraps of debris, but those aside, the pasture showed no sign of the tragedy enacted amid its grasses on that fog-shrouded day in 1945.

The Proctor crash site

VISITING THE SITE

Having sought permission, the site is a 500 yard walk from Knotlow Farm, itself served by a track at SK 11242 76646, off the High Peak-Hargatewell Road.

Sheffield

8. Republic F-84F Thunderstreak 52-6692
Lodge Moor Hospital, Sheffield

SK 28745 86183 290 m
Unit and Station: United States Air Force in Europe (USAFE),
20th Tactical Fighter Bomber Wing, RAF Station Wethersfield, Essex
Date: 9 December 1955
Crew: pilot, successfully ejected, slight leg injury:
First Lieutenant Roy G. Evans, USAF
Casualties on the ground: Hospital patient Mrs Elsie Murdoch, died of
injuries. Seven other patients suffered minor injuries and shock

During the afternoon of 9 December 1955 First Lieutenant Roy G. Evans,
on the attached strength of RAF Wethersfield, took off from the American
Air Force base at RAF Sculthorpe, near Fakenham, Norfolk, on a solo
instrument-flying sortie. After some time, however, and while he was
penetrating cloud, his engine failed, or in jet terminology, 'flamed out'. He
at once began a series of attempts to get the engine going again – to 're-light'
it –, all to no avail. Inexorably losing height, he called base, but received no
answer, almost certainly because he was over a hundred miles distant and
already descending through three thousand feet. Finally, forced to concede
that his Thunderstreak had now become an extremely inefficient glider, he
transmitted blind, declaring that he was abandoning, and ejected.

Colonel Harold Bailer, of Base Operations, Burtonwood, later told the
press, 'We could just faintly hear Lieutenant Evans, but he could not hear
us. "I have a flameout – leaving the aircraft", that was the last we heard of
him.' Adding, somewhat unaccountably, 'We couldn't quite get what he was
trying to say.' (Bringing to mind the semi-jocular pre-take-off cockpit brief,
'If I say "Eject" don't say "What?" or you'll be talking to yourself.')

The ejection was successful although Lieutenant Evans suffered a
slight leg injury on touching down. Once retrieved – he was just east of

Hathersage –, he was taken to the American Air Force base at Burtonwood, where he was hospitalised for a number of days.

When he had ejected, Lieutenant Evans had been in cloud and over open country. Unbeknownst to him, however, Sheffield had been filling the horizon immediately ahead. So it was that the aircraft, weighing by that time some 25,000 pounds and now become a flying missile, overflew some four miles of inviting open moorland before impacting upon Lodge Moor Hospital on the western extremity of the city.

The crashed Thunderstreak amid the wreckage of Ward North One

There were many witnesses. 'It was five o'clock in the afternoon,' Mr Charles Leech, of Redmires Road, told the newspapers, 'when the plane roared over the first hospital building and crashed into the second. I saw flames, and ran across the road to help. It was in two parts, blazing furiously, and ammunition was going off.'

Similarly, Mr Selwyn Williams, of Lodge Moor Road, told reporters that, having phoned 999, he arrived at the aircraft to find that: 'Its tail was leaning against the wall, and a number of people with blackened faces were running about …' In fact, the rear section of the airframe had come to rest by the hospital mortuary, while the burning engine was only yards from the ambulance station and its thousand-gallon petrol store!

Hospital porters were among those who braved the flames, even penetrating to the cockpit, well aware of, but selflessly setting aside, the risk from exploding ammunition, intent as they were on seeking to extricate the pilot they expected to find trapped within. 'Don't make me out a hero,' protested porter Mr George Littlewood, when later singled out for commendation, 'we all did no more than our duty in the circumstances.'

And the burning wreck aside, circumstances were horrendous. For although the aircraft had missed striking the lofty hospital water tower, and had overflown many of the twelve single-storied cubicle blocks, it had then struck the roof of Ward North Two, demolished the interlinking glass corridor, smashed through a sanitary block into Ward North One, then breaking in two, had burst into flames in the quadrangle beyond.

The track flown by the abandoned Thunderstreak

In its progress through the building, moreover, it had left seven hospital patients with injuries which later needed treatment. Of the cubicles the aircraft actually tore through, the first had only moments before been vacated by a nurse, Mrs Margaret Schoefield, and a patient, taken to get a cup of tea. Tragically, the second, and adjoining one, contained the hapless Mrs Elsie Murdock, of Sheffield, mother of a family, and due for discharge. Nurse Schoefield, steadfastly collecting herself, clambered back into the now ruinous cubicle, only to find that her patient had received mortal injuries to her head. Yet amid all the turmoil and confusion, with detonating ammunition zipping through the air, and flames threatening a secondary explosion at any moment, Nurse Schoefield remained with Mrs Murdock, comforting her until she died, only then leaving the danger area to tend to the living, patients and staff alike, many of whom were traumatised and in need of her assistance.

Shocked though the staff understandably were, they clearly behaved in exemplary fashion, for by the time the hastily-summoned fire service had extinguished both the fires, order had been re-imposed, with patients having been re-allocated to undamaged wards. Nor were the patients unappreciative, youthful Nurse Shirley Taylor being deservedly eulogised as 'the little nurse of North Two'.

The Hospital Board paid their own tributes, bestowing formal thanks upon those members of staff whose conduct had been brought to their notice. In the aftermath, too, the local member of parliament approached then-Prime Minister Anthony Eden, taxing him to ensure that USAF and RAF aircraft were not armed as a matter of course, but only when engaged in active live-firing exercises.

An American board of inquiry generated a report comprising 480 pages with 15 photographs and for the next few days *The Sheffield Independent* duly recorded the names of the high-ranking officers and their entourages who processed through the hospital, not least, 'two colonels – one bringing his wife along too – from Burtonwood.'

Two official statements were made by USAFE. The initial one admitted baldly, speaking of Lieutenant Evans, 'We have no idea what caused him to eject himself. We think he ejected at 2,500 feet. He has very minor injuries'. But subsequently, having observed of the F-84 Thunderstreak, 'It is a one-man aircraft and only well-qualified pilots are allowed to take them up,' the spokesman went on to tell the press, 'the aircraft crashed after it apparently ran out of fuel.'

Tragic as the occurrence was, one must spare a thought for Lieutenant Evans, for how wretched he must have felt on hearing what had happened!

Elated at his own survival, he must then have plumbed the depths. Especially knowing that a mere nudge of stick and rudder would have faced the Thunderstreak with open moorland!

Although the area has been considerably altered, former Acting Matron Mrs Diane Couldwell, of Redmires Road, was able to point out where the aircraft had finished up, so providing the co-ordinates.

VISITING THE SITE

Private houses now occupy the crash site, so nothing is to be seen, only the water tower.

9. Hawker Audax K5132
Coal Aston (alternatively Norton) Aerodrome, Greenhill, Sheffield

SK 35473 81352 179 m

Unit and Squadron: No. 11 Flying Training School, RAF Shawbury, Shropshire, No. 23 (Training) Group, RAF Flying Training Command

Date: 7 February 1939

Crew: pupil pilot, Corporal William W. Thompson, shocked

On 7 February 1939 pupil-pilot Corporal William Thompson, a trainee with some 128 hours' flying experience, which included 60 hours on the Audax, was dispatched on a solo, night cross-country flight from RAF Shawbury, in Shropshire. In the course of this flight he went off track but eventually re-located himself over Sheffield. By that time, however, his fuel was running low, so, realising that he was some sixty-five miles from his base, he decided to make a precautionary landing on a former World War One landing ground maintained as an aerodrome by Sheffield Corporation. During the First World War the landing ground had served No.2 Northern Aircraft Repair Depot which, situated between Coal Aston to the south and Norton to the north, was confusingly designated as both Norton and Coal Aston. The depot had been centred upon the crossroads of Norton Lane and Dyche Lane, and in the 1914–18 War its landing strip had been equipped with a flare path. By 1939, however, this aid, and indeed the greater part of the site buildings, had long gone, presenting Corporal Thompson with the daunting task of setting down with only his wingtip flares for illumination.

The Norton Aerodrome site

Fortunately, Mr Cedric Rotchell, the motor mechanic in charge of the night shift at nearby Mssrs Newboult and Sons Garage, on Meadowhall Crossroads, realised that the pilot circling low overhead wanted to set down. As he told the *Sheffield Telegraph*, 'I drove my car to the airfield and put my headlights on to assist him. I was then joined by Mr R. Neale, of Overstones, Norton Lane, who switched on his headlights too.'

It seems that the additional lights gave Corporal Thompson the visual reference he required, for he now made his third approach. Seeing a tree looming up, however, he hastily banked aside but in doing so hit the ground short of the strip, his aircraft overturning and catching fire. As the newspaper quoted Mr Rotchell, 'He seemed to lose height suddenly, and dropped like a stone. The plane's nose struck the ground and it turned right over. A verey light set fire to the wing [in fact, a wingtip landing flare] and at the same time the engine burst into flame. I climbed up onto the wing and shouted to the pilot. At first he did not answer. Then his head came out of the cockpit and he said he was alright. He climbed out and fell semi-conscious to the floor. Aided by Mr Beale and PC Price, I dragged him away from the flames. I asked if there was anyone else in the plane but he replied that he was alone. He was badly shaken, but didn't appear seriously hurt.' Fellow rescuer Mr Neale expressed his admiration for the selfless way in which Mr Rotchell had gone about helping the pilot. 'He deserves a medal,' he told reporters.

The Audax crash site

VISITING THE SITE

Mrs Sheila Gilmour, of the Norton History Group, explained that Norton College now stands at the intersection of Dyche Lane and Norton Lane, and that the broad dual carriageway of the Bochum Parkway which actually parallels Norton Lane now swallows the crash site itself. Just the same, the area beyond the Parkway, and to the front of Norton College, will represent a close-proximity site for the suburban walker.

10. Bristol BE2C
Near Coal Aston (otherwise Norton) Aerodrome, Sheffield

Exact site undetermined
Unit and Squadron: A Flight, No. 33 Squadron,
Royal Flying Corps Station Coal Aston
Date: 24 September 1916.
Crew: Pilot, slightly injured

• Captain E.N. Clinton, Royal Flying Corps

Norton (Coal Aston) Aerodrome, on the 'tween-wars AA Register

On 24 September 1916 Captain E.N. Clinton was detailed to carry out a night patrol, the duty of RFC Coal Aston being to protect Sheffield's industries from air raiders. After flying for some thirty minutes in poor visibility, he attempted to put down – what necessitated this is not recorded – but crashed into high ground and was slightly injured.

11. Unspecified type, Royal Flying Corps
Near Coal Aston (Norton) Aerodrome, Sheffield

Exact site undetermined
Unit and Squadron: Delivery Flight, No. 2 Northern Repair Depot,
Royal Flying Corps Station Coal Aston
Date: 10 August 1917
Crew: pilot, fatally injured
• Captain H.E. Dixon, Royal Flying Corps

On 10 August 1917 Captain H.E. Dixon was tasked to deliver a machine to its designated unit. Shortly after taking off from the No. 2 Northern Repair Depot at RFC Coal Aston, however, he crashed, suffering injuries from which he died a week later. The type of aircraft involved is not recorded, but machines dispatched from Coal Aston in 1917 included RE8 corps-reconnaissance aircraft, and FE2b and BE12 two-seater fighters.

12. Gloster Meteor Mk.8 WE916
Silkstone Road, Frecheville, Sheffield south-east

SK 40477 83801 127 m
Unit and Squadron: No. 211 Flying Training School, RAF Worksop,
No. 25 Group, Flying Training Command
Date: 26 May 1955.
Crew: pilot, killed
* Pilot Officer John Alexander Cohen

Pilot Officer John Cohen, a pupil pilot at No. 112 Flying Training School at RAF Worksop, had logged just under 300 flying hours, including some 50 hours on Meteors, when he was authorised to carry out a night training sortie. In the course of his flying training he had been assessed as 'Average' – that is, perfectly satisfactory –, and had already proved his ability to fly with reference to instruments alone, having acquired a White instrument rating card. This was a significant step up from the Basic instrument rating, indeed it was the working instrument rating for many first-line squadron fighter pilots of the day who never spent long enough in cloud to claim the Green or Master Green ratings. Just the same, Pilot Officer Cohen had only flown the Meteor for some five hours at night.

Having got airborne at 2300 hours he settled in with some circuit work, touching down and then getting airborne again without stopping. Next he climbed to 20,000 feet, as briefed, to carry out a controlled descent through cloud, a cloud-break procedure designed to keep him clear of all high ground during his descent while putting him into a position from which he could see the airfield, then visually join the circuit and land. The cloud conditions on this particular occasion, layered to 12,000 feet with a base of some 1,500 feet, meant that the procedure would be, for the most part, a real cloud-break procedure rather than a merely simulated one.

Pilot Officer Cohen climbed to height, and called for the homing which began the procedure. Worksop's air traffic control descended him to 18,000 feet while bringing him to their overhead, then turned him onto the safe lane which ran slightly north of west (290° magnetic). Now heading away from Worksop, he was cleared to descend to 10,000 feet. Pilot Officer Cohen acknowledged his clearance and indicated that he was commencing his rapid-rate descent: holding descent speed with throttles closed and airbrakes extended.

As expected, some two minutes later he advised that he was approaching 10,000 feet and turning left, that is, back towards Worksop. This was acknowledged by the controller and an easterly inbound heading passed of 100° magnetic. The anticipated next call was Pilot Officer Cohen's confirmation that he was now descending on that heading. When no such confirmation was received the controller began calling Pilot Officer Cohen. Except that there was no reply, although the calls were continued until the news was received that the aircraft had crashed.

It was discovered that, moments after his last transmission, Pilot Officer Cohen's Meteor, still some thirty degrees off its assigned inbound heading, and still in a steep descent, had plunged into open farmland in a suburb of Sheffield and exploded fierily in a deep crater. Pilot Officer Cohen had not attempted to (manually) abandon his aircraft and had been killed on impact.

The investigation proffered the cause of the accident as loss of control during the descending left-hand turn, a quite demanding, and potentially disorientating manoeuvre when done at a rapid rate of descent, on instruments, at night, and almost certainly, in this instance, in cloud. However, as the holder of a White instrument rating, it should have been well within Pilot Officer Cohen's capabilities. Therefore all the senior officers up to and including the Air Officer Commanding in Chief, expressed the opinion that there was not evidence enough to determine the cause of the accident, and further, that no responsibility could be fixed. Not a satisfactory result, but the best that could be arrived at.

The aircraft had, it transpired, plunged into farmland at the end of Silkstone Road, Frecheville, startling many people who had stayed up late listening to the election results in which Anthony Eden had been returned. Others, woken by the sound of the crash, were thrown into alarm. One, a St John's Ambulance man, leaped from his bed, hurriedly wrapped a macintosh around himself, and ran from his house to help. To discover nothing but a smoking, twelve-foot deep crater from which the pilot's body would later be recovered.

Frecheville crater

The crash scene

2013 photo-match of the crash scene

Mrs Ivy Potts, of Silkstone Road, remembered the night vividly. 'It was gone eleven, and we were in bed,' she recalled, 'when we heard this screeching sound, like a bomb coming down. Then there came a terrible crash. We both ran downstairs, and from our front door we could see these flames in the fields at the bottom of the road.' She gestured down the road towards the corner. 'Of course, there were no houses then, the road finished at the junction with Silkstone Crescent, and there were no trees and bushes. My husband joined the people already running down there, but he found there was nothing to be done. Fortunately, working in the mines, he was used to gruesome sights, so what he saw didn't upset him unduly. But, of course, the poor young man was killed. And some days later his parents came to see where he had died: it was all very tragic.' And in another facet of the tragedy *The Times* recorded that Pilot Officer Cohen had recently signed as wicket keeper and batsman for Glamorgan!

Mr James William Hill, also of Silkstone Road, who had spent four wartime years in Burma, working on an earlier generation of fighter aircraft, on Spitfires and Hurricanes, was able to point out the site. 'I didn't see it for some time after the crash,' he observed, 'but the area's quite different now, for it was good pasture then, with none of this undergrowth.'

VISITING THE SITE

There is limited opportunity-parking at the end of Silkstone Road, the site being just 200 feet into open ground, but with shrubs, brambles, and dog walkers abounding.

North Anston

13. Short Stirling Mk.1 W7467
Corner Farm, North Anston, Sheffield

SK 51459 84424 94 m initial impact point, on railway
SK 51272 84235 91 m terminal impact point
Unit and Squadron: No. 149 Squadron, RAF Mildenhall,
south-east of Ely, No. 3 Group, Bomber Command
Date: 16 January 1942
Crew: eight, seven parachuted and survived, captain successfully forced
landed. (Other than the pilot, the crew categories, not being known,
are assigned on the assumption that the Air Britain source listed them
according to the traditional crew hierarchy)

- Acting Flying Officer W.G. Barnes, pilot
- Sergeant Baker, observer (navigator)
- Sergeant Townsend, bomb aimer
- Sergeant C.W. Dellow, flight engineer
- Sergeant Heron, wireless operator/air gunner
- Sergeant Crook, wireless operator/air gunner
- Sergeant F.T.P. Gallagher, air gunner
- Sergeant Collins, air gunner

On 15 January 1942 No. 149 Squadron, stationed at RAF Mildenhall, was
tasked to dispatch its Stirlings to raid Hamburg. Among the aircraft taking
part was Stirling W7467, under the command of Acting Flying Officer
W.G Barnes, who was logged as getting airborne at 1823 hours. His crew
successfully reached and bombed their target, but while still over Hamburg,
and in the process of turning away, amid the flak, searchlights, incipient
mayhem and confusion, they suffered a simple engine failure, which must
surely have required them to exercise the qualities encapsulated in their
squadron motto of –'*Fortis nocte*': strong by night – given that any of them
even knew of the motto, the serving RAF never having been unduly attuned
to Service history.

To employ the phrase 'nothing daunted', seems problematical, for such a stroke of untoward misfortune must have rocked any crew, notwithstanding which the aircraft was turned onto a heading for home. The crew might well have hoped for clear weather conditions as they neared their Suffolk base, but the night was not yet to go their way, for, finding themselves in conditions of very reduced visibility, they droned the time away, fruitlessly trying to locate themselves, until eventually the fuel state became critical.

At 0208 hours Acting Flying Officer Barnes advised control that he had made the decision to abandon the aircraft, after which all seven members of his crew made successful parachute descents. It is not known why Acting Flying Officer Barnes himself did not follow suit, although one wonders if a natural reluctance to leave a still controllable aircraft was not complemented by a concern that once he left his seat the Stirling, although trimmed to compensate for its asymmetric state with him at the controls, might then heel over, generating aerodynamic forces that would prevent him from exiting. As it was, he seems to have elected to bring the bomber in for a precautionary landing.

How he went about this must remain a puzzle, for not only was the blackout in force but a seasonal low-level fog was exacerbated by the then-inveterate industrial haze drifting eastwards from Sheffield. Whether Acting Flying Officer Barnes saw it or not, the field that presented itself to his descending machine, it transpired, was at Corner Farm, North Anston, a full hundred miles from Mildenhall. True, he clipped a railway embankment, skipped a field, then finally touched down for good, careering on across fields and a brook before coming to a halt. But against all the odds, he survived with just minor injuries. Certainly, when daylight came he was found in his seat, fast asleep.

The aircraft, however, was very badly damaged and in the next few days was removed by Queen Mary trailers accessing the site from the A57.

Railway embankment struck by the Stirling's undercarriage

Stirling terminal area

To Mrs Grace Waller, of Hardwick Farm, Todwick, the incident still seemed fresh. 'We were living at Corner Farm, North Anston, at the time,' she said. 'I was fifteen, and was sleeping with one of my sisters when we heard this terrific noise. If there had been an air-raid siren Dad would have made us go to the barn: it only had a relatively-light pantile roof, whereas to have the stone house come down on us would have been a different proposition. But the siren hadn't sounded. And once the roaring sound had passed, there was silence. The whole family crowded to the landing window, but there was nothing to be seen outside. It was dark, of course, but also it was foggy. And in those days they were real fogs, for we were downwind of Sheffield with all its factory chimneys, so that folk said you could only see Sheffield when it rained. Once it was light, and we heard about the plane, Dad decided we'd go and see it before morning milking. We found that it had come from an eastwardly direction, somehow managing to miss the high part of the village by descending with the slope of the ground. Evidently it had come over Corner Farm, skimmed our front field, just touched the railway – there was a definite mark on the embankment –, then actually come down on its belly in our back field. It had left great skid marks – we followed them through the fog. Then it had gone down the slope to Anston Brook, somehow negotiated the far bank of that, but in doing so had been spun to one side, so that it finished up facing towards South Anston.'

She smiled, indicating the site. 'Of course there were no trees then, and even the Brook was different. But back then the first person to find the plane was one of Turner's men who had taken his plough team into the field, only as he worked towards the railway so this great aeroplane took shape in the mist. In fact, he found the pilot had either stayed in his cockpit, or gone back to it, and was asleep. For my part I remember the great belts of bullets which had fed the guns.

We'd come from the direction of the farm, of course, and so we got quite close. The bobby from South Anston, though, was stopping people coming from the road – the A57 – and was annoyed when he eventually saw us. He shouted for us to go away. "But it's my field," my father yelled back. Just the same we weren't allowed to get too close. And soon the Home

Guard came, and eventually, the RAF. In the end they brought long trailers into the field, dismantled it – it was very big – and took it away. And that's really all we ever found out about it. We heard that the crew had baled out near the coast, but we never really knew.'

The RAF crash report summary does not actually mention the crew, or specifically detail the way in which Acting Flying Officer Barnes set about landing the aircraft in the pitch dark. But then these were pragmatic times, and the bare minimum sufficed. After all, the bomber had done its job before being wrecked, and once its captain had recovered, its crew was fit for future operations. But in all conscience, Acting Flying Officer Barnes can have had no idea what sort of terrain he was descending into. Ironically, the area beyond the crash site, towards Todwick, was so flat that parts of it had been earmarked for Sheffield Airport, a scheme successfully fought off as far back as 1933. Yet his aircraft's belly must have been unbelievably close to the ground as he descended over the highest part of North Anston.

What does occur that Mildenhall is only 33 feet above sea level. Which means that as the railway embankment came up Acting Flying Officer Barnes' altimeter would still have been reading 300 feet. It is almost certain then, that what interrupted his gentle descent was an utterly unexpected touchdown a good three hundred feet early! Certainly, however false Lady Luck may have played him over the target, she certainly atoned for her capriciousness when she set him safely down at North Anston.

VISITING THE SITE

The terminal site can be seen from the A57, but both sites can be accessed after parking in the village, beyond Main Street.

Thorpe Salvin

14. Bristol Fighter
Little Wood, Thorpe Salvin

SK 52061 80369 107 m
Formation: RAF
Date: 1927–8
Crew: pilot unhurt
- Unidentified

This incident, in which the Bristol Fighter, short of fuel, merely put down, was refuelled, and then took off again, hardly represents a crash, but it is certainly evocative of the 'Golden Age' of flying of which H. Barber had written back in 1916 in '*The Aeroplane Speaks*' when he has his pilot observe, 'Well, it's a fearful bore, but the first rule of our game is never to take an unnecessary risk.' [A homily delivered as, standing close beside his aircraft, the pilot puffs at his lit pipe!] The set-down also forms one of the earliest aviation memories of Mr Bert Waller, of Hardwick Farm, Todwick.

'It happened in 1927 or 1928,' he recalled, 'when we were at Moor Mill Farm. A Bristol with a great radial engine came down beside Little Wood. He'd been on his way to Nottingham and had run out of fuel. So they got four gallons of petrol in cans, and filled him up. I was very young, but Jack Apple, who worked for us, took me along with him. I walked as far as I could, then Jack put me on his shoulders for the rest of the way. It had come down just beside Little Wood. And once it was refuelled it took off again. But seeing it so close whetted my appetite, so that, in 1934, when Scott and Black won the Melbourne Air Race, there was an air show at Netherthorpe, and I took my savings, didn't tell anyone, and bought a ten minute flight in a Bristol for five shillings [25p].'

Mr Waller smiled, 'I also remember helping push the first plane back onto Netherthorpe aerodrome: it's always been rather short.'

The set-down site of the Bristol Fighter, beside Little Wood

15. Cessna 150, G-BFSR
Thorpe Common, Thorpe Salvin

SK 52687 79417 92 m

Operator: Netherthorpe Aerodrome

Date: 9 December 1978

Occupants: two, both unhurt:

- Mr Paul Harrison, assistant flying instructor
- Mr Phillip Waller, student pilot

On 9 December 1978 Cessna 150 G-BFSR, engaged in flying training from Netherthorpe Aerodrome, suffered an engine failure shortly after take-off and was badly damaged when it made an emergency landing in a ploughed field. Neither occupant was hurt.

Mr Phillip Waller, student pilot

Mr Phillip Waller, of Todwick, the student pilot, described the incident. 'Having done about twelve hours flying, and been solo, I was doing dual consolidation. I'd carried out the take-off and we were climbing through about 600 feet when the engine cut dead. My instructor, Mr Harrison, took over, kept straight, and put us into a ploughed field – White's Field. But the earth was soft, with just a light covering of snow, so the moment the nosewheel touched, it dug in, and the tail flipped over, leaving us inverted.

Fortunately, although this particular Cessna wasn't approved for aerobatics, it had a four-point harness fitted, as opposed to a lap strap, and so we were held securely in our seats. Mind you, it took a very long minute and a half before we could release ourselves and climb out. The aircraft was very substantially damaged, particularly the wings, but after that I rather lost track of it. Certainly it was dragged from the fields, but whether it flew again I don't know. They suspected carburettor icing, but were unable to substantiate it.'

And how did Mr Waller feel, as a raw-enough student, having an aircraft let him down like that? 'We had a very good Chief Flying Instructor,' he explained, 'Wendy Mills, and she had me up again less than an hour and a half later.' After which, Mr Waller progressed very well and achieved his Private Pilots Licence.

With Netherthorpe aerodrome carrying out flying training in the vicinity it is hardly surprising that such incidents occur, albeit infrequently. Even so, two men survived similar crashes on 10 May 1991, and 1 March 1996 respectively. Both though, occurred to the east of the Three Shires Stone, the point at which Yorkshire, Nottinghamshire, and Derbyshire meet. As the Cessna crash site is to the west of the Stone, however, and as the modern Derbyshire boundary marches with that of its forbear, ancient Mercia, the Cessna site is justly included as the most easterly of all those covered in this series.

The Cessna impact area

Kiveton Park

16. Vickers Armstrongs Wellington Mk.10 MF633
Red Hill, Kiveton Park, south-east of Sheffield

SK 49898 82909 110 m
Unit and Squadron: No. 201 Advanced Flying School (AFS),
RAF Swinderby (near Newark), No. 21 Group, Flying Training Command.
Date: 29 June 1951
Crew: three, all killed
* Pilot Officer Thomas Andrew Blair Bond, pilot
* Flying Officer Ryland Leonard Luffman, navigator
* Sergeant Bernard Leslie Curson, air signaller

Despite the comprehensive process by which the RAF has selected them, one of the prime concerns of the majority of pupil aircrew has always been that, having started training, they will fail to meet the standard and be 'chopped'. As a corollary of this, when a fellow pupil is suspended from training, and particularly if 'the chop' falls towards the end of the course, it is invariably felt that a pupil so keen might surely have been given just that little bit more time in which to improve. Yet for instructional staff the decision to continue training in doubtful cases is a fine one, and with the best will in the world, the wrong decision is sometimes made. Sadly for all concerned, this seems to have been the case on 29 June 1951, when Wellington MF633 of No. 201 Advanced Flying School, RAF Swinderby, near Newark, was lost with all three members of its trainee crew.

Pilot Officer Thomas Bond and his crew were returning from a four-hour night cross-country exercise, the final one of their course, and having advised air traffic that they would reach Swinderby in six minutes, were homing on a bearing. Moments later, their aircraft emerged from cloud and crashed at Red Hill, Kiveton Park, near Sheffield, catching fire and killing everyone on board.

MF633 crash site

Boys viewing the scene

The alarm was raised by Mr Oswald Ilsley, Kiveton Park's grocer, who phoned 999. Other witnesses later testified to having seen the aircraft break cloud with both engines going, then make a steep right-hand turn in the course of which the nose dropped and the aircraft spiralled into the ground.

The investigators quickly turned their attention to the bright lights of Kiveton colliery. After which, having collated all the evidence, they deduced that, regardless of the fact that his navigator's estimate had placed him a good five minutes from Swinderby, Pilot Officer Bond, on breaking cloud, had immediately assumed that the lights below were those of the airfield and commenced a robust turn. They further deduced that as he tried to reconcile the lighting pattern below with what he expected to see at Swinderby, he had become disorientated, lost control, allowed his turn to steepen into a spiral dive, and crashed.

When he died, Pilot Officer Bond had done a total of 277 hours solo flying, including 23 hours on Wellingtons, twelve hours of night flying, and in addition, 45 hours practising instrument flying on the Link trainer: all noticeably higher than might have been expected for a pupil at that stage of training. His record also showed that he had made heavy going of the course. 'Throughout training,' the court of inquiry revealed, 'the pilot has made erratic progress and at best only reached low-average standard. He appears to have been of highly strung and nervous disposition.' And they added a note, 'Pilot's reaction to emergency open to doubt.'

But it goes without saying that Pilot Officer Bond would have been keenness itself to carry on and to eventually achieve his goal – the RAF motto specifies *Per Ardua*, after all! And clearly his aspirations had persuaded his instructors to permit him just those few hours more. Poor fellow! Poor hapless crew! Yet the understanding of even the higher echelons showed through in the rider they added to the findings of the court that 'no blame [is] attached to [the] instructors for persevering with [the] pilot's training.'

Mr Len Gibson, of Wales, adjoining Kiveton Park, an RAF corporal engaged in crash and recovery duties at the time of the accident, was sent to carry out an independent inspection of the team detailed for the task and recalled that because one of the engines was over twenty feet down, it was left there.

The Red Hill Wellington site, 2013

VISITING THE SITE

Mr Jack Clark, occupier of a bungalow built only yards from where the Wellington struck a tree then sprayed the slope with debris, pointed out the impact point, explaining, 'But the houses on Dandy and Trinity Roads have been built over the whole area.'

17. Unidentified Type
Kiveton Hall Farm, Kiveton Park

SK 49828 83210 120 m

Date: c.1936

Having spoken about the Wellington crashing on Red Hill at Kiveton Park (see above), Mr Jack Clark tendered, 'But that wasn't only bit of aviation history hereabouts, for in 1936 a passenger plane put down into the field at Kiveton Hall Farm. It was one of those which carried about eight in its cabin, and it had either got lost or run short of fuel. But although the field was big enough for it to land in, it couldn't be taken off again. Or perhaps it had been damaged. But after a day or so it was taken away by road. As for the type, I couldn't say, I probably didn't know even when I went to see it. But it wasn't a biplane.'

The set-down area, Kiveton, c.1936

Todwick

18. Gloster Meteor Mk.4 VW267
Todwick, Sheffield

SK 48572 84100 97 m

Unit and Squadron: No. 92 Squadron, RAF Linton-on-Ouse,
Fighter Command

Date: 14 May 1950

Crew: pilot, killed

- Squadron Leader Raymond Hiley Harries, DSO and bar, DFC and
  two bars

On 14 May 1950 Squadron Leader Raymond Hiley Harries took off in
Meteor Mk.4 VW267 to return to Linton-on-Ouse from Biggin Hill, where
he had been a guest of the officers' mess. In the course of the flight he ran
out of fuel, and was killed when his aircraft crashed at Todwick ['Todd-
ick'], near Sheffield, after he had failed in his bid to manually abandon,
the Mk.4 having no ejector seat. It became clear to the investigators
summoned to the scene that, once Squadron Leader Harries had left the
cockpit, his parachute canopy had become entangled with the tailplane.
Indeed, a Royal Observer Corps (ROC) post in Nottinghamshire had
reported a Meteor passing overhead in a shallow dive with its pilot
dangling in its wake. The unmanned – but banefully encumbered –
aircraft, eventually dived into fields beside a copse at Todwick, locally
known as The Meadows, or alternatively, The Oscars, and was seen, in
its last few moments of flight by, among others, Mr Les Waller, later to
become a parish councillor.

'We were returning with a load of asbestos,' Mr Waller explained,
'which I'd begged for a local community project from the redundant RAF
radar station nearby. We heard this jet coming, and just as we turned in
towards the park so it dived out of the sky straight into a field. It exploded
in flames on impact and there were bits everywhere, all across the field,

some very gruesome. But close though we had been, the police got there before we did. They kept us well back, and then the RAF arrived.'

Mr Len Gibson, to become a long-time resident of nearby Wales, had an even more intimate association with the crash. 'At the time,' he recalled, 'I was a corporal with No. 64 Maintenance Unit, RAF Rufforth, and engaged in crash-recovery duties. On that Sunday afternoon I was returning from a liaison visit to Air Ministry when I was taken from the train and driven straight to the Todwick site. I was told not to worry about accommodation, that my billet had been fixed.' He smiled at Margaret, his wife. Who smiled back. 'And he's still here, all these years later.'

Mrs Gibson then recounted her own experience of the crash. 'I was making bread, and had just taken the loaf from the oven when the Meteor crashed. And the whoompf! and the concussion made me throw the lot into the air! But it was worse for my friends, John and Cynthia Thompson, who were courting at the time, and were on the main Wales road when the aircraft flew overhead, for when they ran across the fields towards it they came upon one of the pilot's legs.'

The former corporal nodded. 'Once at the site I found that the aircraft had impacted in quite a shallow dive, finishing up with its nose semi-buried and both wings fragmented. There was no cockpit canopy, the parachute was tangled around the tail, and it was clear from the state of the pilot's body that he had been out of the cockpit at the time of the crash. It was a hideous sight, and an even more hideous scenario, even though our medical officer reckoned he would have been, at best, in and out of consciousness.'

'Yet local people,' Mrs Gibson put in, 'used to believe that the pilot had been trying to climb back aboard up the lines of the parachute!'

Mr Gibson was able to furnish a first-hand picture of the work of RAF salvage and recovery crews between 1946 and 1956. 'In this case', he explained, 'we used a Coles Crane to pull out the concertinaed wreckage, being very careful when we got to the cockpit, for that was where we were most likely to find clues, looking for, and reporting, anything that seemed out of place. Here, it was evident that the pilot had been on a "jolly", for jammed down beside the seat we found golf clubs and balls, and golf shoes, all damaged.'

'In fact,' he expanded, 'our task was wide-ranging, for we didn't only categorise crashed machines but also carried out a variety of repairs, although big jobs would be taken to the maintenance unit at St Athan. Regarding clearing the sites, if aircraft parts had buried themselves deeper than twenty feet we could get permission to leave them, otherwise our responsibility was to clear up every bit of metal, taking particular care if the land was to be grazed upon. To that end, the team leader would liaise with landowners and obtain a clearance certificate to show that their land had been fairly restored. In fact, he'd do all the paperwork, arranging compensation and the like. And always, there would be the press. Our official brief was to make no statements to them at all, but unofficially the line was, "Tell them anything; just get rid of them." '

And the conveniently arranged billet? 'Strange as it's seemed since,' Mr Gifford confessed, 'the whole week I was in the house I didn't even notice the daughter … not until I'd left …' At which his wife gave a quiet chuckle.

The crash, as a non-operational accident, had an especial irony in that Squadron Leader Harries, a pilot with some 1,700 hours experience, had begun his flying career in the Battle of Britain and then survived four years of operational flying, downing a total of 24 enemy aircraft and gaining for himself the Distinguished Service Order and bar, the Distinguished Flying Cross and two bars, and the *Croix de Guerre* from both the French and the Belgians.

In view of Squadron Leader Harries' illustrious record it was doubly unfortunate that the court of inquiry had no option but to be uncomplimentary, unequivocally finding that the primary cause of the crash had been a 'lack of firm pre-flight briefing by [the] pilot.' For Squadron Leader Harries had embarked upon a thirty-five minute flight with fuel enough for just forty minutes, and not having assimilated that the destination homer was unserviceable, had then steered a heading which took him significantly left of the track for Church Fenton, the crash site being fifteen miles off that track.

He had, of course, expected to be flying at high altitude, except that the oxygen bottles had not been topped up before departure. Then again, he had known before takeoff that a critical channel on his radio was unserviceable. Just the same, having been airborne for 39 minutes, at which time he was flying at just 6,000 feet, a height at which a jet engine would simply guzzle its paraffin fuel supply, he did manage to advise Church Fenton that he was baling out due to lack of fuel.

In fact, the picture that emerges of this tragic flight lends credence to the story, apparently current among the members of the crash team at the time, that the officers' mess at Biggin had proved to be rather more than just a little too hospitable. The kindest the Air Officer Commanding in Chief could allow, however, was to record that the accident had been caused by 'Pilot's error of judgement'.

Mr Richard Waller, at the impact point of Meteor VW267

VISITING THE SITE

Goosecarr Lane leaves the A57 at SK 48509 85294. Just before entering Todwick, turning right onto Storth Lane permits access and parking close to the site. As might be expected on a working farm, there is no trace of the tragic finish to this ill-conceived flight. Just the same, Mr Bert Waller, of nearby Hardwick Farm, found debris as late as 2003.

Treeton

19. Bristol Fighter Mk.3 J8458
Manor Woodlands Farm, Treeton Grange, Rotherham

SK 44289 87326 87 m, area of
Unit and Station: No. 2 Flying Training School, RAF Digby
(Lincolnshire), Inland Area
Date: 22 September 1930
Crew: pupil pilot, mortally injured:
• Pilot Officer Alfred Cecil Sant

On 22 September 1930 Pilot Officer Alfred Sant, a pupil pilot at an advanced stage of his flying training at RAF Digby, was authorised for a solo return cross-country flight to RAF Upper Heyford, in Oxfordshire. The outbound leg was uneventful, but on his return flight Pilot Officer Sant's navigation went awry and he realised that he had progressed too far north. Ascertaining that he was near Sheffield, thirty miles off track, he calculated a new course, and turned onto a south-easterly heading. Unfortunately, at this juncture his engine began giving trouble.

The machine, a Bristol Fighter, had been air tested at Digby by instructor Sergeant L.C. Marks before Pilot Officer Sant had been allowed to take it up, but it is not known whether this had been a routine check, or whether it was to confirm that an engine fault had been corrected. As it was, the farmer at Manor Woodlands Farm, Treeton Grange, Rotherham, was convinced that the approaching machine was in trouble.

'He came from the north-west,' he told the local newspaper, 'flying very low, with his engine misfiring. Indeed on one or two occasions it stopped altogether, at which the pilot decided upon landing in one of my fields. He made a good touch down, and when I reached him he told me that his magneto had begun missing. On finding that the nearest telephone was at the colliery, four hundred yards away, however, he began to examine the engine himself. Once he started it up again, though, it seemed to be running very slowly. Just the same, he got the people who had gathered to turn the machine into wind, and said he would "take it for a low run". He sat there with it going for about two minutes, then set off towards Aughton [to the south-east], getting up after about fifty yards and flying at fifty or so feet. But just as he reached the next field, the engine – which had been sounding very rough indeed – stopped short. Then the plane keeled sharply to the left, dived steeply, and burying its nose in the ground, spun about to face the way it had come. We rushed to it, to find the front badly damaged, the lower left wing totally destroyed, and the propeller yards off, stuck into the soil. The pilot was obviously in a bad way. Indeed, we had to cut one of his shoes away from the rudder bar before we could free him. Even so he died two days later in Rotherham hospital.'

At the inquest, a Flight Lieutenant White, sent from RAF Digby to assist the coroner as a specialist witness, advised that the Bristol Fighter's fuel system had both a priming pump and a hand-operated pressure pump, and that having been on the ground for some time, it would have been necessary to employ the hand pump before take off. He felt it only too likely that Pilot Officer Sant had not remembered to do this, and had, therefore, regardless of any other problem, starved his engine of fuel.

Mr Hedley Frost, of Treeton, remembered that the detached propeller had stood in a local house for many years. 'Though it's long gone now, I suspect.'

Bristol Fighter location, Treeton

VISITING THE SITE

Manor Woodlands Farm has become a housing complex, while the smaller fields of the day have been merged into a single enormous stretch, making it virtually impossible to determine exactly where the set-down and subsequent crash occurred: even Mr Frost could only venture that it had been somewhere in the general area of Treeton Grange and to the north of Wood Lane. The reference given, however, does meet the additional criteria of being some four hundred yards from the colliery.

Ringinglow

20. Fairey Battle Mk.1 K9221
Dore, south of Ringinglow

SK 28939 82668 351 m
Unit and Squadron: No. 16 (Polish) Flying Training School,
RAF Newton, near Nottingham, Polish Air Force under British Command
Date: 28 August 1941
Crew: pilot, uninjured
- Leading Aircraftman Leon Pszeniczka, pupil pilot,
  Polish Air Force under British Command

When the single-engined Fairey Battle monoplane light bomber entered
RAF service in 1937, a post-design extra crew position and other
modifications had so added to its weight that, when matched against
modern fighters and ground anti-aircraft defences, it proved disastrously
slow. Following a series of debacles, each a harrowing saga of gallantry, the
type was withdrawn from operations in September 1940 and relegated to
the training role.

So it was that on 28 August 1941 Leading Aircraftman Pszeniczka,
airborne on a solo navigation and map reading cross-country, was transiting
the Parkhead area in the south-west of Sheffield when the engine of his
Battle caught fire. An unenviable situation for any pilot, and one in which
many might have taken to their parachutes without further ado, let alone a
pupil with just fifty hours behind him. Indeed, the contemporary training
manual urged personal safety as the first consideration, with loss of the
machine very much secondary. Notwithstanding which the young Pole put
his aircraft first, and decided to do his best to save it.

Ruddering into a descending spiral – to deflect the fire with yaw – he
evidently followed the recommended drill, turning off the fuel, pushing the
throttle fully open until the engine stopped, then, in turn, flicking off the
ignition switch and operating the fire extinguisher. 'Evidently', for at that

point Fortune, having had her little jest, favoured him, and saw to it that the drill killed the fire.

The procedure necessarily cost him height, but with no more flames to menace him he came out of his skidding turn and banked towards a suitable-looking area of open moorland, just beyond the closely-walled pastures of a farm. Then, still sticking to the approved procedure for the tailwheel aircraft of the day, he carried out a neat, wheels-up belly landing, the upward slope and the rough ground bringing the aircraft to an abrupt, but safe halt.

Among those who witnessed the drama was Mr Noel Hancock of Sheephill Farm, Ringinglow. 'He came from the direction of Sheffield,' he recalled. 'He was on fire, I could see. But he made two circles, and then came down on his belly onto Houndkirk Moor, just beyond our boundary.' And Mr Hancock smiled, remembering how he, his slightly older brother, Roy, and their dog, had run to the scene. 'Our mother was frantically calling us to come back, telling us that the pilot might be a German. But we took no notice, and just ran faster.' His smile broadened. 'Mind you, while we ran we did agree that if he really turned out to be a German we'd turn and run straight back again.'

How quickly they would have returned to mum had they heard the Polish guttural is a matter for speculation, for when they reached the boundary wall they stopped, all three, and merely peered over, the dog on its hind legs.

'The pilot was standing by the aeroplane,' Mr Hancock continued, 'all covered in what looked to be oil, but was probably smoke. We were the first on the scene. But then lots of people began arriving.'

Another resident, to whose cottage Leading Aircraftman Pszeniczka was led for succour, remembered the aircraft remaining on the moor under guard for some time before it was removed. 'It was hardly damaged, so there was little enough left once they'd gone,' the lady said. However, the locally-proffered story of a subsequent romance between a girl from the cottage and the young Pole was strongly denied …

To explain Leading Aircraftman Pszeniczka's presence in Britain it is necessary to remember that Britain and France had given guarantees to

Poland. Accordingly, on 1 September 1939, when Germany invaded Poland, the guarantee was called into play, and two days later both Allies declared war on Germany. Swamped by superior forces the Poles resisted bravely, and when the hoped for – and it must be said, trustingly expected – help from their Allies did not materialise, they told themselves that at least they were holding down one front of the common fight. But when Russia treacherously launched its own pincering invasion two weeks later, the Poles knew the end had come. Acting on orders from their Government, as many Servicemen as possible crossed into then-neutral Romania. From there, after a nominal period of internment, they were moved to France, and when France fell, on to England, clamouring to be allowed to fight alongside the British armed forces. For expediency, the airmen among them were enlisted into the RAF Voluntary Reserve, but swiftly-consulted legislation soon sanctioned the setting up of 'The Polish Air Force under British Command'.

Before the invasion of Poland Leading Aircraftman Pszeniczka had been serving with the Polish Sixth Air Force Regiment, and on arrival in Britain had continued his interrupted pilot training. However, despite the aptitude he showed in handling the fire-in-the-air situation and the subsequent forced-landing, things evidently went awry at some later stage of his flying training, for he failed to gain his pilot's wings, and in 1943 remustered to become a ground Radio-Telephony Operator.

Fairey Battle site

VISITING THE SITE

The site, on rough moorland, shows no sign of the incident and although Mr Hancock personally directed searchers, metal detectors turned up nothing. The area, though, on the Ringinglow moorlands, is well worth visiting.

21. Bristol Blenheim Mk.4 Z5746
Ox Stones, Ringinglow, west of Sheffield

SK 27883 83214 420 m

Unit and Station: RAF Catfoss, near Hornsea (East Riding of Yorkshire), No. 2 Operational Training Unit, No. 17 Group, Coastal Command

Date: 26 January 1941

Crew: three, all killed

* Sergeant John Robson, pilot
* Pilot Officer Ivor King Parry-Jones, navigator
* Flight Sergeant Eric Brown, wireless operator/air gunner

By 1941 even the updated Mk.4 Blenheim had been withdrawn from active operations in Europe. Long before that, though, many had been diverted to other roles, notably to training, and to units like No. 2 Operational Training Unit, whose function was to produce crews for Coastal Command.

But training had its own risks, as on 26 January 1941 when Sergeant John Robson and his trainee crew were carrying out a navigational exercise and strayed from their course into an area of high ground. With their altimeter still set to register the height above their sea-level base, they flew into a 1,380 feet above sea level, gently rising moorland at Ox Stones, near Ringinglow, all three dying from the impact.

The crash had been heard in Ringinglow, consequently would-be rescuers were quickly on the scene. Only to discover that nothing could be done. In the aftermath the recovery teams arrived with their Queen Mary trailers and took away the wreckage.

The investigation found that the accident had been caused by an error of navigation, surmising too that the aircraft had been in cloud when it crashed. The Air Officer Commanding, when the findings were passed to him, made the additional, and transparently political, point that the orders for the flight – issued on his authority, of course, by his subordinate commanders – had been adequate, and that the pilot had been specifically instructed to turn back if the weather became unsuitable.

Mr Kenneth Wilson, of Hathersage, whose sheep were to range the Ox Stones area for many years, was able to verify the impact site. 'Peter Priestley,' he said, 'of Overstones Farm, an early arrival, likened the plane to a big bird on the snow. It seemed quite whole, only when he tried to get closer he was stopped by a soldier who said he was a sentry. "Then tha's a long way off tha' post," Peter told him, sure that the chap had crept off for a pint.'

Of additional interest to aviation-minded walkers, Mr Wilson was also able to point out the moorland site, off the Houndkirk Road (at SK 77700 81400), of one of the decoy-Sheffields, where piled motor tyres were set ablaze when German bombers were expected. 'But,' he said, a little wryly, 'they never wasted a single bomb on Houndkirk.'

The Blenheim crash site, near the Ox Stones

VISITING THE SITE

The closest parking is in the lay-by on the Ringinglow Road at SK 27892 83470, after which the site is just 300 yards into the moor towards Ox Stones: a feature hidden by the rising moor and itself sufficient reason for leaving the road! However, with the aircraft having bellied onto only gently rising, snow-covered moorland, it shed little debris on its slide, the flourishing heather offering little chance of even fragments being found.

22. Miles Master Mk.1 T8324
Burbage Rocks Edge, Upper Burbage Bridge, near Hathersage

SK 25803 80805 320 m
Unit and Station: No. 5 Elementary Flying Training School,
RAF Ternhill, Market Drayton, No. 21 Group, Flying Training Command
Date: 26 March 1941
Crew: pupil pilot, killed
• Leading Aircraftman Edward John Marsland Atherton,
  RAF Volunteer Reserve

On 26 March 1941 pupil pilot Leading Aircraftman Edward Atherton was airborne on a solo navigational exercise when he became lost, wandered off his planned and approved course into a hilly area, and struck the cloud-covered high moorland to the north-east of Hathersage. Leading Aircraftman Atherton was killed and the aircraft was destroyed by fire.

Mr Robert Stamper, of Hathersage, recalled, 'When news came that this trainer had crashed, Police Constable Ron Kirby – Rip, as we called him – detailed the policeman we had lodging with us, PC Gateskill, to bike up and mount guard on it. When PC Gateskill came back, though, he was very upset. The plane having burnt out, a mortician from Sheffield had set his mallet-wielding assistant to straighten out the blackened body of the pilot. But what they evidently regarded as an everyday process was altogether too much for our lodger. There was nothing he could do, however, but grit it out, and get on with standing guard duty.' Mr Stamper paused, and reflected. 'I can't remember going up there myself, but the wreckage was soon cleared.'

Mr Kenneth Wilson, of Greenwood Farm, on the other hand, not only remembered visiting the crash site as a lad but also discussing it with author Ron Collier many years later. As he described it, 'The aircraft had crashed between the railed-off [1927-vintage] water gauge and the Edge, just yards into the moor, and may well have burned, but there were pieces of tubing, and the like, which I took for souvenirs and kept for ages. In fact, I went back there in the mid-nineties, and there were still pieces sprinkling the ground beneath the heather.'

The impact site, just short of the railed-off c.1927 water gauge, looking towards Upper Burbage Bridge

Mr Wilson, too, remembered the Hathersage police presence in the shape of the redoubtable PC Kirby. 'He'd carry home eggs from the farms in his helmet,' he smiled. 'And when some Germans had gone missing from Lodge Moor prisoner-of-war camp, he checked a barn, and seeing their feet protruding from the hay, had the farmer march them down to the police house with his shotgun. Then, after the army had collected them, he confiscated the gun because the farmer lacked the proper wartime licence.'

Mr Stamper, for his part, was able to provide a photograph vividly portraying wartime Hathersage, showing him among a group of Hathersage schoolchildren scrabbling about in one of the three bomb craters along the Sheffield Road. (Bombs held locally – as ever – to have been 'jettisoned by a German bomber' which was then shot down into the sea.)

Hathersage children in a bomb crater

VISITING THE SITE

Having parked at Upper Burbage Bridge, the site is 410 yards, south-eastwards, along the Burbage Rocks Edge.

Foolow

23. North American Harvard Mk.2B FX306
Foolow, north-east of Tideswell

SK 18674 76837 291 m

Unit and Squadron: No. 6 Flying Training School, RAF Ternhill, Market Drayton, Shropshire, No. 23 Group, Flying Training Command

Date: 10 December 1952

Crew: pupil pilot, seriously injured:
- Pilot Officer Ronald Windle

Although unsophisticated, the Harvard was a demanding machine – arguably the reason it proved such a good advanced trainer. Certainly it required its pilot to be cognisant of both its handling qualities and its technical foibles, as one pupil, Pilot Officer Ronald Windle, was to discover on 10 December 1952.

The morning was dull, but perfectly fit for flying, and Pilot Officer Windle was duly sent solo from RAF Station Ternhill. His brief was to carry out circuits and landings together with local map reading, the latter an exercise which, unlike a formal cross-country, did not necessarily call for detailed pre-flight navigational planning.

Once airborne, Pilot Officer Windle elected to scout the local area to the north-east, evidently intending to leave the circuit work until the end of the detail. However, after just over an hour without radio contact he was heard to call for navigational assistance, reporting that his engine was running unevenly. Ternhill Air Traffic Control were unable to establish two-way communication with him and directed another of the unit's aircraft to act as an airborne link, a measure, as it turned out, that brought no results.

Even as this was going on, however, people at Tideswell, some forty-six miles to the north-east of Ternhill, were watching Pilot Officer Windle circle the town at a relatively low altitude in an evident attempt to determine his position visually. They then heard his engine cut, upon which they saw him head off eastwards in a straight glide. A glide which ended when he touched down in a pasture on the western outskirts of Foolow village, bumping over a series of sizeable hummocks before violently striking a drystone wall. Unhappily, both his seat and his harness attachment-points broke away on impact with the wall, so that he was thrown forwards and seriously injured.

Salvage crew at the Harvard

The subsequent inquiry established that Pilot Officer Windle's engine had been perfectly serviceable, the rough running having been an indication of fuel starvation. The operating procedure was to switch over the tanks if rough running occurred, but as the warning had not been assimilated by the pilot, and the reselection had not been made, the engine had simply stopped dead.

Further, while conceding that Pilot Officer Windle's radio jack-plug had probably been intermittent, the inquiry found that he had been flying at such a low altitude as to effectively cut himself off from both radar and the navigational assistance he had sought.

Pilot Officer Windle had 69 hours' solo experience but he had trained in uncluttered Canada, so it was understandable that he had become lost in trying to map read in poor visibility and over terrain so full of detail; he was, after all, still a pupil.

Presumably then, with so much seeming to crowd in upon him – as indeed it had been –, the basic desirability of touching down into wind must have fled from his mind. Accordingly, caught at relatively low altitude when his engine had cut, he had not attempted to set up an emergency pattern, but had glided directly on until he was forced into a downwind – and therefore, at a wind-enhanced, higher-speed – landing.

Just the same, it was very bad luck that, due to the hummocky nature of the far end of the pasture, both seat and harness-attachment chose to break just as Pilot Officer Windle nosed into the wall. The injuries he received, though unspecified in the accident report summary, were severe enough to render him unfit for further RAF service and he duly relinquished his commission on 15 March 1954. It would have been small comfort to him, then, that the accident led to a modification of the seat and the harness securing-points, and that Flying Training Command's contemporary apportionment of solo flight and dual supervision was questioned.

Harvard crash site, 2013

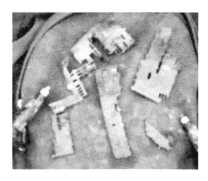

Debris unearthed, battery plates

VISITING THE SITE

Approaching from the Hucklows (the west), the crash site is to the left of the narrow, bendy road, just before entering Foolow. The rocky hummocks which so unsettled the final part of Pilot Officer Windle's landing run have long been excavated away and the land refilled and re-turfed, with, at best, only the unearthed fragments of the aircraft's battery being lodged in a wall. Very careful opportunity parking can be found near the site, but perhaps best to carry on, and enjoy the pastoral tranquillity the village offers.

24. Vickers Armstrongs Wellington Mk.1C DV732
Eyam Moor, eastern end of Sir William Hill Road

SK 22285 78097 373 m

Unit and Squadron: No. 11 Operational Training Unit, RAF Westcott, Aylesbury, No. 92 Group, Bomber Command

Date: 2 June 1943

Crew: five, all survived, uninjured

- Sergeant R. H. Trangmar, Royal New Zealand Air Force, pilot
- Other crew members unidentified

Long before October 1943 when the Wellington was withdrawn from bombing operations over Europe, it had proved its worth as a training aircraft, and from then on it was to become the mainstay of the Operational Training Units (OTUs) preparing aircrews for both twin- and later, four-engined first-line bombers. Similarly the machine had proved its dependability. Yet dependable and worthy as the type was, the all-year-round production of crews, many of whom had done their basic training over the uncluttered plains of Canada or Rhodesia, always had inherent risks.

This was well illustrated on 2 June 1943 when, at 0230 hours, in the course of a night-navigation exercise, Wellington DV732, was flown into high moorland above the celebrated plague village of Eyam. Although none of the crew sustained any injury, the aircraft had to be written off.

The court of inquiry submitted that Sergeant Trangmar, of the Royal New Zealand Air Force, had simply flown into the hillside in the dark. The finding, subsequently concurred with at all levels, was that bad navigation had caused the aircraft to be off track, and that it had been flying 'unnecessarily low'. The Air Officer Commanding encompassed the whole as, 'bad captaincy'.

Mr John Hancock at the site, on Eyam Moor

Mr John Hancock was able to point out the site, tramping the heather much as he had done sixty years before. 'I was about fourteen,' he said, 'and cycled over here with friends. The Wimpy was pretty whole, although the trellis-like geodetic showed through where its back had broken. And the nose was somewhat skewed off.' He indicated the skyline ridge, descending from the nearby trig point, 'How on earth it missed that! But I suppose it was already in a shallow easterly descent, for there was hardly a mark on the heather back along its way, no furrow or anything. It must have simply have brushed it, and slowed, until it actually struck.' He smiled. 'We were able to look around inside. But so little had come off it that all I took away was a piece of perspex.'

VISITING THE SITE

The crash site is in flourishing heather and hardly fifty yards from a public footpath. Mr Hancock commented on how little the aircraft had fragmented, while the proximity of the (much effectively unpaved) Sir William Hill road would have eased the salvage task considerably. Having parked, though, there is splendid walking hereabouts …

Dronfield

26. Taylorcraft Auster
Toad's Mouth, Hathersage

SK 25803 80805 320 m
Operator: Flying club aircraft
Date: 1950–60s

Toad's Mouth Auster site

This incident was recorded in a generally dependable enthusiast list compiled in the 1970s. Lack of detail notwithstanding, the occurrence is included here against something more coming to light in the future. Certainly, there would have been coverage in the local press.

26. Taylorcraft Auster
Owler Bar, south-west of Sheffield

SK 29402 77921, 299 m

Operator: North-East Airways

Date: 8 January 1951

Crew: pilot, unhurt

• Captain G.S. Pine

On 8 January 1951, when Captain Pine, of North East Airways was flying from Brough, near Hull, to his base at Blackpool, he was caught out by bad weather in the vicinity of Sheffield. Well aware of the high ground he would have to overfly, he judicially put his Auster down at Owler Bar. The field he chose, directly opposite the Peacock Inn, and paralleling the elongated roundabout, was adequate to the purpose, but a slightly undulating surface caused his propeller to strike the ground, breaking off one of the tips. The aircraft remained on the ground for a day or two until the engine was checked for internal damage due to the impact, but once reassured on that score, and after a replacement propeller had been obtained and fitted, Captain Pine then flew the aircraft onwards to his base.

The incident was reported in the *Sheffield Independent* newspaper on 9 January 1951, together with a photograph of the downed aircraft and its pilot. Unfortunately the original plate was not retained by the paper and the print is too poor to usefully reproduce.

Mr Howard Fisher, of Pewitt Farm, near Owler Bar, recalled, 'It came down in the field opposite the Peacock. There wasn't much wrong with it. And after a day or so, it flew off again.'

An innocuous enough incident. But one imbued with the flavour of the new, post-war attitude to flight safety, the captain setting his machine down rather than risk low-level flight through cloud-obscured hills.

Captain Pike's set-down field

VISITING THE SITE

Nothing to see, but on leaving Owler Bar there are fine moorlands on one side and fine woodlands on the other …

27. Vickers Armstrongs Wellington Mk.2, Z8491
White Edge Moor, north-east of Froggart

SK 26987 77406 358 m

Unit and Squadron: No. 12 Squadron, RAF Binbrook
(south-west of Grimsby), No. 1 Group, Bomber Command
Date: 6 February 1942
Crew: six, five injured

- Flying Officer Colin Arthur Barnes, DFC, pilot, broken ankle
- Sergeant Jack Seamen, second pilot, on operational experience, frostbite
- Sergeant Bob Coldwell, navigator, minor injuries
- Sergeant Brian Lunn, bomb aimer, concussed
- Sergeant 'Kit' Carson, wireless operator, minor injuries
- Sergeant John Blute, air gunner (rear turret)

The ruggedness that helped many Wellingtons limp home despite severe battle damage, also helped save some of those crews who found themselves unexpectedly brought to earth. Certainly Flying Officer Colin Barnes, DFC, and his crew found cause to thank that basic robustness of the Wellington on 6 February 1942, when they were dispatched from RAF Binbrook, near Grimsby, to the westernmost extremity of Brittany to bomb German installations at Brest.

The round trip would have taken the No. 12 Squadron crews some four and a half hours, but as Wellington Z8491 neared Brest it became obvious to Flying Officer Barnes that thick cloud was going to prevent them from identifying the target. True, by 1942 there would no longer have been any restriction on their dropping, or even jettisoning, their bombs anywhere over Germany if faced with such conditions, but indiscriminate bombing over Occupied France was unthinkable, consequently he aborted the operation, and keeping his bombs on board, faced about for home.

On making a landfall in the region of Start Point, the crew still had some 265 miles to go to reach Binbrook. But as it was a route they had so recently transited they were familiar with the weather pattern and would have had as up-to-date a wind as any. So, although it was a seasonable February night, with low cloud, no moon, and with the blacked-out ground made even more featureless by deep snow, the flight would have presented no problems. Accordingly, they seem to have settled onto their north-easterly heading and patiently awaited the navigator's estimate for Binbrook.

The lapse time to Binbrook would have been some eighty minutes from leaving Start Point, so that with ten minutes to go – representing thirty-five miles – they would have anticipated being in the area of Newark. Which meant that the only terrain of note ahead was the Wolds, a ridge of low hills nowhere that much higher than Binbrook, itself standing at a mere 370 feet above sea level. Surely then, there was no danger in easing down through the cloud? And no reason at all for breaking W/T radio silence, or bothering any emergency service, even the HF 'Darky' get-you-home organisation.

Except that as they commenced their descent, and with their altimeter still reading some 1,200 feet, they struck the ground. The aircraft bounded high, struck again, then, having hung as if suspended for long seconds on end, impacted for a final time, only now with such violence that it broke its back. Providentially, there was no fire, nor did the bomb load detonate, despite a main ordnance comprising seven 500 pound bombs.

The crash, by former Sergeant Carson, courtesy Mr Roni Wilkinson,
Pen & Sword

Once those who were able to had managed to scramble clear it was found that the tail had twisted, rope-like, then come to rest fin downwards. However, despite the basic integrity of the rest of the machine, a hasty muster failed to account for two crew members. Air gunner Sergeant John Blute was quickly located in the tail turret, but there was no sign amidst the wreckage of the second pilot, Sergeant Jack Seaman.

With that mystery shelved for the present it was found that Sergeant Blute, although uninjured, was trapped upside down in the turret from which, despite all efforts, the crew were unable to extricate him. For the rest, the captain, Flying Officer Barnes, was now immobilised with a broken ankle, and bomb-aimer Sergeant Brian Lunn, who had been stationed in the front turret, was concussed.

Eventually, although with everyone still at a loss to account for the second pilot, some sort of order was established, and Sergeant 'Kit' Carson, the wireless operator, and the only one presently capable of the undertaking, was dispatched to try to summon assistance.

Not surprisingly, Sergeant Carson found the going tough, having to force his way across pitch-dark, heather-choked, and largely hummock-grassed moorland where the footing was made yet more treacherous by deep snow. Nor were these the only hazards, for when Mr Bill Sayles, the resident water inspector, spotted him from his doorway, the airman, heading for the water-control tower, dimly silhouetted against the whiteness, was perilously close to blundering onto the only thinly-iced Barbrook Reservoir.

The Sales' Home, from which the rescue effort was launched

Sergeant Carson was swiftly handed into the care of Mrs Margaret Sayles while Mr Sayles set about organising a search party. Indeed, it is to be hoped that the family received some recognition for their night's work, for in addition to organising the rescue, Mr Sayles himself made two forays to the crash site, first leading rescuers, then assisting a crew member back.

The trapped gunner was eventually released and along with the others remaining at the site was escorted down the moor to the house. But only later, as the day drew on, was the missing second pilot discovered. He had been thrown clear, it transpired, and being badly shocked, had assumed that he was, in fact, in Occupied France, after which, taking to heart his escape-and-evasion lectures, he had lain low until daylight. He was found to have cracked ribs, with frostbite subsequently costing him some fingers.

But not least among the casualties was to be an unidentified member of the local Home Guard who, gallantly making over his greatcoat to one of the crew at the crash site, then fell victim to exposure, from which he was never to fully recover.

Just a few days later the bombs had been disposed of and the site cleared of all wreckage. On the administrative side, similarly, the inquiry worked swiftly. They were reporting, after all, on an operational sortie, and operationally-qualified crews were precious commodities. Accordingly, the Binbrook Station Commander merely noted that, in his opinion, his pilot had 'lost height thinking he was over low country'. Nor was there anything but the tiniest suggestion of mild reproof in the investigators' summary that the aircraft, 'Flew into high ground owing to navigational errors in bad visibility'. Consequently, with the inquiry's findings submitted and approved, the incident was closed.

With their injuries healed, and having had their survivors' leave, the various crew members went their separate ways. Sergeant Lunn and Sergeant Blute were later to be killed on ops. As was Sergeant Coldwell, although by then he had – in chronological progression – been awarded a Distinguished Flying Medal, been commissioned, reached the rank of flight lieutenant, and received a Distinguished Service Order, the latter no mean distinction for an officer so junior. Sergeant Seaman flew on as a captain in his own right, surviving the war, while, with his ankle mended, Flying Officer Barnes transferred to instructing on Heavy Conversion Units, eventually leaving the Service as a squadron leader.

But that night in February 1942 was not quite the last Flying Officer Barnes was to see of White Edge Moor. For after the war he returned, by daylight, and accompanied by his wife, and walked out to the crash site where he duly photographed his lady standing beside a singularly-kinked sapling with Barbrook Reservoir as a backdrop.

The kinked tree, still a useful locater for the terminal site in 2013

Then again, Sergeant Carson, the erstwhile wireless operator of Wellington Z8491 who also survived the war, painted the machine as he remembered it from that night, twisted, battered, and buckled, tail awry, but with its integrity not essentially compromised, for all that it would never fly again.

And yet for many years it did seem that Z8491 might well have taken wings once more, for no physical evidence of an impact site had been found despite exhaustive searches. In August 2005, however, Mr Ken Adlington, of Shepherd Flatt Farm, generously driven onto the moor by Eastern Moors Estate Warden, Mr Danny Udall, was able to throw light on the lack of debris.

'At the time of the crash,' Mr Adlington explained, 'I was Head Shepherd for the Water Board, who owned the moor. First thing next morning we followed the wall from the "Grouse Inn" to the Hurkling Stone and then to a spot adjacent to the single tree to where the main wreckage was. Beyond that there were two scars a few hundred yards back where it had touched and bounced – on a line back towards where the trig point is now. The Wellington had obviously descended over White Edge, but then come down where the ground flattens, touching a time or two before finally stopping, breaking its back to leave its tail resting on its fin.'

He reflected. 'I can't remember seeing any bombs, but then on that first visit the Holmesfield Home Guard had gone and the army were there – busily pointing their rifles! After that a salvage gang dealt with the wreck; they weren't in uniform. A friend of mine, Richard Crossland, had a Fordson tractor, the only one in the area, and as the wreckage was dismantled it was dragged off the moor and along the Reservoir walls to the access road near the Swales' house. As for the lack of debris since, people took souvenirs at the time, of course – in particular, I remember the two of the gamekeeper's sons from White Edge Lodge, nothing was too big or heavy for that pair! –, so there wasn't a nut or bolt left – an absolutely swept-up job.' But he then produced a tiny fragment. 'Even that,' he said, just a little wryly, conscious suddenly, it might be, of the passage of time, 'I probably picked up thirty years ago, for it must be that long since I've been out here ...'

Former Shepherd Ken Adlington, and Estate Warden Danny Udall at the terminal site

Ken Adlington, with a scrap of debris. Also a section of fuel pipe, found by the author.

VISITING THE SITE

Parking can be found in a lay-by at Barbrook Bridge (SK 27576 78299) on the B6054. A track then leads for just over half a mile to the Hurkling Stone (SK 26946 77723). After which the terminal site is 340 yards off on 173°M. In early 2013 'the tree' was still there, while deer were nowhere near as scarce as aircraft debris.

Mr Ken Adlington.
Ken was to die within days of passing on the exact location of this site, at that juncture, information only he still possessed. Which makes this an opportune place to pay grateful tribute to all those who, in furtherance of this research, supplied knowledge that, by dint of time, only they were still party to, and by 2014 were no longer with us.

Chesterfield Area

28. Bristol Blenheim Mk.4 V6078
Spitewinter, north-east of Matlock

SK 34332 66203 277 m

Unit and Squadron: No. 42 Operational Training Unit, RAF Ashbourne, No. 70 Group, Army Co-operation Command

Date: 7 April 1943

Crew: three, all killed

- Pilot Officer John Barry Welton, pilot
- Sergeant Leslie Harold Redford, navigator/bomb aimer
- Sergeant Eric Desmond Murphy, wireless operator/air gunner

At the start of the Second World War it was generally accepted that the RAF had a world beater in the Blenheim. In truth, however, technical development had been so swift that the type was effectively redundant from the outset. Just the same, the Blenheim continued to give good value as a trainer, and it was in that role that Blenheim V6078, of No. 42 Operational Training Unit, was dispatched from RAF Ashbourne on 7 April 1943.

Pilot Officer John Welton and his crew were tasked to carry out a night navigation and wireless-telegraphy (W/T) cross-country. This meant that the wireless operator/air gunner, Sergeant Eric Murphy, was expected to play a key part in the conduct of the flight by furnishing weather information, directional bearings, and fixes. The court of inquiry, however, was to establish that the aircraft had set course without having done either a ground or an airborne check on a W/T equipment which subsequently proved to be unserviceable.

The corollary of this was that when, during the course of the flight, the inexperienced crew realised that they had became totally lost, the pilot took up the pre-planned heading for base and descended through cloud in an endeavour to fix their position. But such blind let-downs are always fraught with danger, and descending far below the safety height for the area, he struck the edge of Scout's Wood, at Spitewinter, north-east of Matlock, and some fourteen miles from Ashbourne. Having lost a wing, the stricken machine rolled violently before plunging, inverted, into the field beyond, the debris spill finishing at a drystone wall. Disintegration was total, and none of the crew survived.

The Spitewinter terminal site; the aircraft first struck the low area in the tree line

One of the earliest would-be rescuers, Air Raid Warden Mr Bill Davis, maintained that the only recognisable part of the machine had been the tailwheel. Indeed, the break up had been so violent that long after the salvage teams had departed, farm workers found themselves retrieving human remains.

Both Mrs Edna Hawksworth (née Keeton) and her brother, Mr John Keeton, whose family farmed the area, and lived just beyond the debris trail, well remembered the night of the crash. 'It was very stormy,' recalled Mr Keeton, 'everyone was in bed, with the windows tightly closed against the wind and rain.' Mrs Hawksworth nodded agreement. 'The aeroplane had hit Scout's Wood, then exploded in the field. But there was nothing to be done ... And they wouldn't allow us children near it.'

Mr Keeton smiled. 'It didn't stop us, of course. For there were souvenirs to be had. Perspex to make into rings, and pendants ...'

Mr Peter Hawksworth, a later incumbent of the farm, remembered his father telling him that some debris – a part of a wing and one of the engines – was left up in a tree. For his own part, he offered, 'And for years afterwards you could see the gap where the aircraft came through the trees, although they've grown up again now. Then, Grandfather found a human jawbone, which he placed in the wall. But I still find bits now and again: of the aircraft, that is ...'

And he produced two items found only months before in the vicinity of the drystone wall.

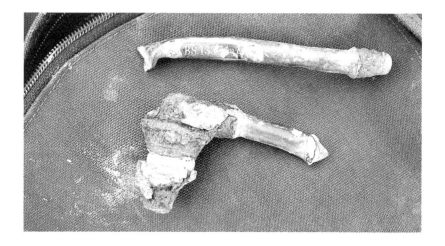

Debris from the Blenheim

VISITING THE SITE

Parking can be found on Highashes Road, abeam the drystone wall, but it is most unlikely that any surface debris will be found.

29. Vickers Armstrongs Wellington Mk.3 X3941
Gladwin's Mark Farm, Screetham

SK 30376 66211 328 m
Unit and Squadron: No. 27 Operational Training Unit,
RAF Church Broughton, No. 91 Group, Bomber Command
Date: 30 January 1943
Crew: five, two killed, three injured:

- Sergeant Kenneth Barton Killeen, Royal Australian Air Force, pilot, killed
- Sergeant William Alan Catron, RAAF, second pilot, on pre-operational experience, killed
- Navigator, wireless operator/air gunner, and rear-turret air gunner: identities unknown, all injured

The basic task of an Operational Training Unit (OTU) was to train aircrews on the twin-engined Wellington, normally prior to further training on four-engined types. No. 27 OTU particularly accommodated Australian crews who had done their training in Canada under the Empire Air Training Scheme and were now being introduced to European flying conditions. Certainly the weather was to prove a prime factor on 3 January 1943 when Sergeant Kenneth Killeen and his trainee crew were dispatched on a night exercise from RAF Church Broughton, a satellite of RAF Lichfield, the parent station of the OTU.

The exercise prescribed was a bombing and navigational sortie known as a 'Bullseye', in which the task was to navigate to, and locate, a target, then to simulate a bombing run by use of photography; although 'Bullseye' exercises might also involve OTU aircraft being sent part-way towards enemy-occupied coasts to lure enemy fighters away from a real raid.

The weather that night, starting as extremely unstable with strong winds and an abundance of rain clouds, steadily worsened, until at about midnight a general recall was issued. Evidently Sergeant Killeen's wireless operator did not receive the message, for there was no acknowledgement.

But two hours later, their detail completed, the crew made contact once again. Furnished with a track to fly, they turned inbound to Church Broughton, and were actually descending. Except that when they were still twenty-two miles short of the aerodrome their aircraft struck a line of trees then plunged into a field. Both pilots were killed, and the other three crew members were injured.

The field was on Gladwin's Mark Farm, Screetham, to the west of Chesterfield, in Derbyshire, but hidden from the farmhouse by a clump of trees. Seeing a flash of moonlight on a distant roof, therefore, the rear gunner, the fittest of the injured men, set out across country, eventually raising the alarm at Mr Lomas' Moor Farm (to become Darley Forest Grange), on Flash Lane, half a mile to the south-west.

Mr David Fearn, a subsequent incumbent, was told how the rear-gunner's arrival was remembered from childhood by Kathleen Lomas, subsequently Mrs Kathleen Dixon, visiting her old home from Australia. 'This German pilot [sic], covered in blood arrived at the door in stormy weather in the middle of the night, giving a terrible fright to my father.'

Farmer Mr Ernest Dronfield could personally vouch for the foulness of the weather that night. 'We'd been to Home Guard in Ashover,' he remembered. 'Farming all day, then Home Guard at night! But what a rum night that was! I never saw such weather: rain, low cloud, and such rough winds! The road to Gladwin's Mark is very exposed but as we turned onto it that night we had to get off and push our bikes. Well, I was only too glad to get indoors and to bed. So I didn't hear about the crash until next day. But then I went over there. I believe they were all Australians ...'

Mr Dronfield was to get to know the wreckage well. 'It crashed in the "Second Ten-Acre field" – some people now call it "Aeroplane" field. The RAF soon cleared the 'plane away. But for years after I was ploughing up bits.' Mr Sam Bown, his step-brother, remembered that too. 'It was 1955 before I started ploughing "Aeroplane" field, but I was always turning up pieces of crumpled aluminium.'

Mr Dronfield resumed his account, 'The 'plane had come from the Chesterfield direction, took the tops off the trees, skimmed over the road and drystone wall, and into the field where it broke up. We always supposed they'd had something wrong with their engines.'

In fact, plotting out the line of flight, from Chesterfield, and beyond the crash site, it becomes clear that Sergeant Killeen and his crew were reasonably on track for RAF Church Broughton. But Mr Dronfield, cycling home, had experienced the worsening violence of the westerly surface wind. It follows, therefore, that the aircraft would have been bucking a significantly-higher headwind aloft. So if the crew had failed to detect the marked increase in wind strength they would not have appreciated the reduction in their speed over the ground. A reduction which meant that they were not as far along the return leg as they had thought. So that as they descended through cloud, thinking they were well clear of any high ground, and with their altimeter showing a comfortable 1,000 feet or so – comfortable for that era, at least –, they would not have expected the ground beneath them to be at just that height above sea level. As, unhappily, it was.

The Gladwin's Mark crash site, looking back along the approach

VISITING THE SITE

Opportunity parking can be found on Screetham Lane at SK 30438 66158. The site, starting some 180 feet inside the field, still gives up debris, not least, fragments of the Wellington's singular geodetic construction, particularly after ploughing.

30. Unidentified twin-engined aircraft
Near Gladwin's Mark Farm

SK 31670 66800 334 m
Date: Late 1939–45

At some stage during the wartime years, a forced, or precautionary, landing was made in the location given, near Gladwin's Mark Farm, Screetham. Research, however, has failed to progress beyond the account given by Mr Ernest Dronfield, of Gladwin's Mark Farm. As a Home Guard he stood sentry over the machine until the duty was taken over by regular troops. As Mr Dronfield remembered, the twin-engined machine – 'a Blenheim, perhaps, or an Anson' – stayed on the ground for two days or so, and was then moved away by road. 'The two chaps in it, though' he recalled, 'were all right.'

Another rather unsatisfactory inclusion, but incorporated, again, in the hope that more details will emerge in the future.

The set-down field used by the unidentified twin-engined type near Gladwin's Mark

31. Handley Page HP54 Harrow Mk.2 K6989
Barlow, north-west of Chesterfield

SK 34350 75192 109 m

Unit and Squadron: No. 214 (Federated Malay States) Squadron, RAF Feltwell, north-east of Ely, No. 3 Group, Bomber Command.

Date: 8 July 1939

Crew: six, uninjured

- Pilot Officer M. F. Briden, pilot
- Identities of the other pilot and three crew members not known

The Handley Page Harrow bomber and troop carrier came into squadron service in January 1937, its design marking the heavy-bomber's transition from biplane to monoplane. Even so, the fixed undercarriage was retained, the Handley-Page justification being that its streamlined design compensated for the weight penalty of a retractable landing gear. Sub-contracting components to many small firms simplified repairs, but neither its rough-field capability nor ease of repair had been able to save Harrow Mk.2 K6989 on 8 July 1939, when it made an inglorious touchdown on its last outing.

This happened after several Harrows of No. 214 Squadron had been on detachment to RAF Aldergrove, Northern Ireland (later, Belfast International Airport), and were returning in company to RAF Feltwell, their Norfolk base, some twelve miles north-east of Ely. While climbing through cloud, however, Harrow K6989, under the command of Pilot Officer M.F. Briden, lost the formation.

The weather was cloudy, and the visibility poor, the high-summer haze being exacerbated by some lingering low-level mist which blotted out much of the ground. Further, in this extremity the wireless operator reported that the communications equipment had stopped working, which meant that the crew was cut off from outside aid. As a result, the time came when Pilot Officer Briden realised that they were hopelessly lost.

While they continued to search for a ground feature with which to fix themselves, Pilot Officer Briden maintained a rough, south-easterly heading for base. As a pilot he was relatively experienced for the day with over three hundred hours on type, if under five hundred hours total flying, and he put all those hours to good use. Eventually, however, with no ground features appearing that would allow the crew to locate themselves by their own efforts, he made the decision to put the machine down in order to ascertain their position before shortage of fuel robbed them of some measure of control.

With forward visibility so much reduced by haze it was, of course, no easy task. Indeed, when he made his first attempt – into a field at the hamlet of Bole Hill, three miles north-west of Chesterfield – he misjudged his approach and lost his tailwheel to some trees.

Hastily going around, he remained in the area, where at least he could see the main layout of the land, finally choosing an upsloping field half a mile to the east, at Barlow, as it would transpire, ninety-eight miles from his base in Norfolk. Only here, in aiming to maximise the space available, he once again brushed through treetops on the approach, this time denting the slipstreaming boots of his main wheels. Even so it seems likely that he feared running out of space after touchdown, for as the speed fell off so he swung the machine diagonally across the field to gain some extra distance. But any such fear proved groundless, and the machine came to rest with space in hand.

The aircraft's arrival was witnessed by Mr Horace Noble, at the time a schoolboy to whom the visitor represented both a welcome break and an outstanding event.

Another witness was villager, Mr Wilf Needham, farmer, special constable, and country-man of many other functions whose oral memories were recorded in the Barlow Social History Group's c.1997 publication, *Everybody is Somebody*. 'We were whitewashing the cowshed,' Wilf remembered, 'when this aeroplane dropped into William Needham's "Seven Acre" field. He had tried to drop at Bole Hill, but had taken off his back wheel. So then he came over the chapel and managed to land in the field opposite the back of David Granger's house. He had broken his undercarriage on some trees at the bottom, and finished facing Chris Holmes' house before turning towards Rutland Terrace.'

Handley Page Harrow K6989, at Barlow. The water plant is to the left

It was clear from the outset that it would not be feasible to make a safe take-off from the field. Therefore, while the crew were driven back to Feltwell, the aircraft was placed under guard, initially by police and special constables, and later by RAF personnel.

The recovery operation was handled by a team from No. 9 Maintenance Unit, but although they officially took over responsibility for the task the next day, the shell of the machine was to remain at Barlow for some considerable time. True, in the contemporary photograph of it on site it appears relatively intact. The accident report, however, records that it had landed heavily: one imagines that the upslope of the field proved deceptive. And evidently the hard touchdown had caused some significant structural damage, for on 30 November 1939 the decision was made to scrap what remained as being beyond economic repair.

'It stayed there for weeks,' Wilf told the history group, 'and became more of a draw for folk that year than the well dressing. So that the hedge all along the lane – the gate, the lot – from Keeper's Cottage, down towards the church, was trampled under by visitors. But when the decision was made to scrap it we got some right good timber. In fact, one piece of three-by-two was used to make the roof of the well dressing.'

But he had apparently remembered with particular satisfaction the oil. 'I asked the sergeant about that, and he said, "If you want it, tek it." So I rushed around the village getting cans to put it in.' Indeed, it is locally held that Wilf was never to actually buy another drop!

Wilf was also to supply a touch of romance involving a well known local family, 'The ginger-haired young lady,' he maintained, 'one of the Helliwells, of Peakley Hill, later married one of the airmen ...'

The Harrow site, showing the water plant to the left

VISITING THE SITE

As the field has been in constant use since the Harrow put down it is hardly surprising that lengthy metal-detector searches produced no evidence. However, the extant water plant furnished a guide for the photo-match map reference supplied here.

32. Miles Master Mk.1 M7836
North Wingfield, near Chesterfield

SK 42256 65307 147 m

Unit and Squadron: No. 7 Operational Training Unit, RAF Hawarden (Chester), No. 10 Group, RAF Fighter Command

Date: 12 October 1940

Crew: OTU pupil pilot, killed

• Sergeant Malcolm Parker

Sergeant Malcolm Parker

The function of No. 7 Operational Training Unit (OTU) was to convert newly-qualified pilots into operational fighter pilots using both Spitfires and Miles Masters. On 12 October 1940, shortly before the unit became No. 57 OTU, Sergeant Malcolm Parker, a student with just under two hundred hours' experience, was briefed for local flying and sent off in Master M7836. Nothing more was heard from Sergeant Parker until the news came in that he had crashed fatally at Highfields, North Wingfield, over sixty miles east of Hawarden.

It was quickly ascertained that Sergeant Parker had lived at North Wingfield, and had deliberately flown there in order to carry out some low-level stunting.

One of the many witnesses of the crash on that Saturday afternoon was miner Mr George Searston. 'It was at about four,' he told *The Derbyshire Times*, 'when I was drawn outside by this very low-flying aeroplane. It flew backwards and forwards several times and was doing aerobatics. It kept coming very low and then zooming upwards. It banked very steeply on occasion, and once or twice it started a loop which developed into a roll. [A layman witness showing a nice eye for a roll off the top!] The last time, after about twenty minutes, it did not come out properly but went straight into a dive, narrowly missing the row of houses and crashing within yards of the railway line with a terrific impact, bursting into flames which were so intense that nobody could get near.'

Mrs Betty Houghton, of Highfields, also had some personal knowledge of aviation, not particularly broad, but noteworthy nevertheless, for as a girl she and two other members of her family had crammed into the back cockpit of Alan Cobham's machine for a joyride during his circus' visit to Ollerton; 'No straps,' she smiled, 'just an open top with the three of us squashed down on the floor.' She remembered the Master crash too, responding immediately, 'Yes, the pilot was Malcolm Parker. And at the time so many people rushed to the crash that they broke down the fencing between the house here, and the railway. In fact, it was my Pop, Arthur Pollett, who brought Malcolm's body to the morgue. Pops worked at the colliery as chauffeur and mechanic, as well as ambulance driver and medical attendant, so he was hardened to grim sights. Just the same, after that accident he was physically sick for days.'

And it had clearly been a grim experience, although Hawarden's medical officer, Flying Officer John Watts, whose transporting aircraft had landed in a field nearby, was able to assure the relatives that Sergeant Parker would have been killed instantly.

Regarding the final moments of the crash, both the coroner and the RAF investigators also heard testimony of a Police Constable Cole, who saw the machine approach from the west and begin its cavortings. From this, together with what miner Mr Searston had told them, they were able to ascertain that Sergeant Parker had eventually pulled up into a left-hand climbing turn but had stalled at an estimated 800 feet, after which the aircraft had spun into the ground and burnt.

The finding was clear, the OTU's commanding officer recording, 'Pilot disobeyed orders – only one hour of local flying had been authorised.' A clear-cut case. Low flying to impress, and thereby destroying an aircraft, and losing the Service a student in the final phase of becoming a useful operational pilot. As the Chief Instructor spelled out, 'disobedience of orders, low flying, and stunting over his house.'

Adding irony to tragedy, Sergeant Parker's display had been watched by his father, who, knowing that his son had progressed to flying Spitfires, had failed to connect him with the trainer!

And yet Sergeant Parker's mother was to suffer even more poignantly, for the RAF accident report particularly notes that the sergeant had been stunting, *'at his mother's request'*. A request made just the week before, during his last leave. Clearly Mrs Parker had admitted as much to the investigators. But what a dreadful burden for her to carry!

Mrs Janet Hague, of Holmeswood, sympathised. 'Edith idolised Malcolm,' she said, 'she was a great Chapel member, and after all, he was her only son.' The stricken mother's regard being amply illustrated by the memorial she erected in nearby Heath churchyard, not settling for the standard Commonwealth War Graves headstone but for a substantial structure of bluish hue, recording that her son was 'Accidentally killed on active service'.

To find this wartime accident reported in the *Derbyshire Times* was unexpected, but gratifying. And it is interesting to note the care taken to blur the facts – in order to 'avoid giving comfort to the enemy', as the contemporary phrase had it. Thus the Master is merely 'a British trainer', Sergeant Parker is stationed 'in the North-West of England', the crash occurred 'in an East Midlands mining village', and his parents, Mr and Mrs William Parker, lived 'in the village near which the plane crashed'; finally, it was explained that 'owing to war restrictions the story of the aeroplane crash was held over from last week'.

The crash-site area, Highfields

VISITING THE SITE

Parking can be found at SK 42017 65448 on the A6175. The crash site, a potato field bordered by the colliery railway at the time, remains farmland, but the railbed is now the 'Five Pits Way', a stile at the first sharp bend from the road offering access to the field. The field was scraped over during reclamation of the colliery site, but local feeling is that the reference given here is very close to the impact area.

33. Unidentified type
Flash Dam, near Screetham, west of Chesterfield

SK 31157 64438
Date: 1939–45

Mr Selwyn Elliot, formerly of the Ordnance Survey, learnt of this widely-sourced incident from his grandfather, who held that it was a light communications machine with 'something hush-hush about it; someone on board who should not have been'. What has been verified is that the location given above was an open quarry at the time, and only later became overgrown with trees and brush. Other sources have the type as both a Magister and a Wellington. The incident is included here against new information coming to light.

Site of the unidentified type at Flash Dam, now overgrown by trees

Stockport

34. Heinkel He111 No.2871 GILH
Springfield Farm, Hazel Grove, Stockport

SJ 94476 87665 122 m

Unit and Squadron: Luftwaffe, *Kampfgeschwader 55*
(KG55: No. 55 Bomber Group),
Soesterberg, Utrecht (Netherlands, due east of Southend-on-Sea)

Date: 8 May 1941

Crew: four, parachuted successfully: one broken ankle, others minor abrasions:

- *Oberleutnant* [Flying officer] Adolf Knorringer, pilot
- *Oberfeldwebel* [Flight sergeant] Karl Kohlhepp, observer/bomb aimer
- *Unteroffizier* [Corporal] Ludwig Rathsam, wireless operator
- *Oberfeldwebel* [Flight sergeant] Aloys Kloos, flight engineer

On the night of 7 May 1941 Heinkel He111 No.2871, based at Soesterberg, Holland, was part of a Luftwaffe force dispatched from occupied-Dutch airfields to bomb targets in the West Midlands. The aircraft was subjected to anti-aircraft fire during its bombing run on Manchester's Old Trafford Industrial Estate – then largely devoted to military production –, and having turned away south-east, towards Stockport, was seen to catch fire. The four-man crew baled out and suffered only minor injuries, and at 0215 hours the burning aircraft impacted and exploded upon open farmland at Hazel Grove. Initially it was supposed, even by members of the crew, that the Heinkel had been hit by anti-aircraft fire, but it was later established that it had been shot down by a Defiant night-fighter.

With a raid in progress over Manchester, Air Raid Precautions (ARP) wardens, fire watchers, and aircraft spotters in the Cheadle, Bramhall, and Hazel Grove areas of Stockport were fully alert, so that not only was the aircraft's fall closely monitored, but the individual crew members were swiftly located, and – very nearly as swiftly – taken into custody.

When British or American aircraft crashed during the Second World War newspapers were permitted to carry little, if anything, of the story. This incident, however, was amply covered by the local newspaper, the *Stockport Express*.

'It was like a streak of fire crossing the sky,' an ARP warden told the paper. 'Suddenly it tilted and disappeared downwards.' After which, as the *Express* described, it touched down inverted and finally blew up as the fuel exploded.

Heinkel He111 No.2871, Springfield Farm

One of the witnesses interviewed by reporters and photographed standing by the main impact crater, was Mr Edward Price, of Cheadle Heath. 'I saw the plane light up as it was hit,' he told them. 'It flew over Cheadle ... and I could see the four men bale out.' He then described how the abandoned machine curved across Bramhall towards Hazel Grove. And he described the scene at Springfield Farm. '[The plane] was scattered all over the place ... covering a couple of acres.' 'A huge area,' as another witness observed.

Then-schoolboy Mr K.J. Daniels of Hazel Grove also visited the site, and in 1978 would write, 'I cycled there the following morning and, risking the attentions of the Home Guard, I obtained some bullets and a petrol cap (which I still have).' Others among the visiting crowds described how the oil covering the ground turned the pasture a dirty yellow.

The crew members, abandoning in disciplined order, the pilot last, fell between Cheadle and Hazel Grove. One broke his ankle on landing, and required an ambulance, but none offered resistance, so that within minutes all were accounted for. Just the same, the treatment accorded one of them by a local dignitary led to controversy. As Mr Daniels recalled when he observed, in 1978, 'I remember the fuss it caused when Councillor Herbert Walls offered "hospitality" to the captured airman.'

The worthy councillor, it transpired, had seen one of the parachutists coming down, and set off by car to capture him, taking with him three other men, among them, as he would argue later, 'An air raid warden, and a high Air Cadet Officer who had a revolver'. Having located and picked up the airman – *Unteroffizier* Rathsam, the wireless operator –, Councillor Walls then decided to take him home to be given first-aid by Mrs Walls – the detracting *Express*, deriding the minor nature of the cuts on the German's lip, nose, and the backs of his hands, observed pointedly, 'but no shrapnel wounds'. The patched-up airman was then regaled with tea and sandwiches. And a full forty minutes after the crash, having confided in the course of chatting that this was his twenty-first birthday, and having displayed personal photographs, he was delivered to the local police station and the authorities.

The *Express* criticised the councillor for departing from government instructions on the handling of downed enemy aircrew. In contrast, it praised the action of two fire watchers who apprehended another similarly injured crew member who was, 'very dazed … and was more afraid than we were'. As the newspaper spelled out, although this enemy airman landed beside their own homes, they very correctly took him to the chief warden's house nearby, to phone for the police.

'The man was lame, and had to be helped to walk,' the men reported. Other than this the airman was virtually cold-shouldered. Even when he asked to be allowed to bathe his bleeding mouth – he had landed badly, on his head, besides losing one of his flying boots in the descent – both men accompanied him into the scullery for fear he would escape. Nor was the shocked flier offered as much as a hot drink, although he was permitted to consume his iron rations, 'a small round tin of chocolate and a few caramels'. Before the police arrived a German speaker had elicited that this had been the airman's third raid over Britain, and that his wife was a nurse.

What made all this the correct course of action, the *Express* pointed out, ignoring the 'inappropriate questioning' (a head under which they criticised the councillor), was that the kinder treatment of the first airman, and the forty-minute delay in turning him over, meant that, with his shock diminishing and his morale burgeoning, he would have been far less likely to give information to the authorities.

In truth, the wrangle smacks rather more of local point-scoring than partisan support for government directives, or fear that evaders might contact fifth columnists, but after exchange and counter-exchange the matter, together with the crash itself, dropped from the news.

The crash, however, was to be resurrected in 1978 when the newspaper called for reminiscences of the incident. An initiative which re-kindled enthusiast interest, for in 1981 an excavation was organised to recover the engines.

Farm owner Mrs Florence Wilkson, who, together with her husband, Roger, came to Springfield Farm not that long after the crash, remembered the preamble to the excavations. 'Mr Hankison,' she recalled, 'was tenant farmer here when the plane came down, and people had often asked to dig in the field for remains. For although there has always been talk of the plane landing on the golf course, just over the hedge, it didn't, but came down in our field. Anyway, in 1981 it was finally agreed. Only when they came to dig they discovered that the engines had already gone.'

Mrs Wilkson's son, named Roger after his father, had known the site all his life. 'We'd frequently plough up bullets, and pieces of aircraft metal,' he recalled. 'But I can't remember seeing anything of note for something like twenty-five years.'

From the start it was assumed that the Heinkel had been hit by anti-aircraft fire, not least because the German wireless operator, as Councillor

Walls reported, 'kept repeating that it was "flack" [*flak*] which brought them down'. However, at least one witness had reported hearing 'what sounded like a burst of machine-gun fire in the distance' before the Heinkel passed overhead 'burning and apparently on one side'. And indeed the kill was claimed by a Defiant night-fighter crewed by Flight Lieutenant Christopher Deanesley, DFC, and air-gunner Flight Sergeant Jack Scott, DFM. In fact, in 1978 the former communicated with the previously mentioned Mr Daniels, confirming that he had been flying a No. 256 Squadron Defiant from Squires Gate, Blackpool, and specifically referring to his 'very skilful' New Zealander air gunner, at that time still resident in Auckland.

No Combat-in-the-Air report has come to light. Therefore the reference to the air-gunner's skill intrigues. For if, as some sources have it, the Defiant's attention was drawn to the He.111 by the anti-aircraft fire, the procedure would then have been for the Defiant pilot to dive beneath the enemy bomber, chancing fire from its single belly-gun, and simply have the gunner rake it from below, paying particular attention to the engines: the *Express* records that in this case some 800 rounds were expended in a diving pursuit, with both the Heinkel's engines catching fire.

Of course, using the word 'skilful' might have been the pilot's supportive way of giving credit to his colleague, crew members – even modern all-important back-seat systems operators – being so often forgotten as media plaudits are heaped upon the pilot.

On the other hand, if the Defiant was one of those equipped with the early form of Airborne Interception radar (AI), the rear-crew member would indeed have had to exercise considerable skill in encompassing the interception, guiding his pilot into an attacking position, and then leaving his radar scope at the last moment, to man his turret, and his guns. Certainly, if such were the case, any publicity would have followed the pattern already set for the kills engineered by Sergeant J.R. Philipson, (and later, navigator Flight Lieutenant Cecil Rawnsley), for their pilot, then-Flight Lieutenant 'Cat's-eyes' Cunningham, when the fable of a carrot diet to improve night vision was invented to screen the existence of the still-classified airborne radar. Nor is it significant that ex-Flight Lieutenant Deanesley did not put the record straight, even as late as 1978, for many ex-servicemen of his era would have held that oaths of secrecy have no term.

As an historical footnote, 8 May 1941 proved costly for the Luftwaffe force sent out against the West Midlands, for two other KG55 machines were lost, together with Junkers Ju88 No.6213, of KG76, the latter coming down in The Roaches. Perhaps it should also be mentioned that one source has KG55's aircraft based at Melun-Villaroche, near Paris, as part of *Luftflotte* (Air Fleet) No. 3, which, if correct, would have faced them with an enormously long flog.

The Springfield Farm site in 2013

VISITING THE SITE

No visual evidence remains, although Mrs Wilkson remembered that for many years there was a faint depression where nettles grew in profusion. This, though, has long been filled in. As it is, the field is often used for haylage [silage – fodder – made from only partly-dried grass], so that although a public footpath borders one end of it, unauthorised incursions onto the unharvested site would be a discourtesy, at the very least.

35. Handley Page
Heyfords

K4868, **SJ 96785 84713** 243 m Homestead Farm, Disley, Cheshire
K6898, **SJ 96805 84619** 197 m The Homestead, Disley, Cheshire
[K4874, Dingle Farm, Oldham, SD 94939 08465 226 m, see *Northern Region, page 136*]

Unit and Squadron: No. 102 Squadron, RAF Finningley
(near Doncaster), No. 3 Group, Bomber Command
Date: 12 December 1936
Crew: K4868, four, uninjured
- Squadron Leader Charles W. Attwood, and unnamed observer, wireless operator, and air gunner
- K6898, four, uninjured
- Pilot Officer Michael George Winsloe Clifford, and unnamed observer, wireless operator, and air gunner

On Saturday, 12 December 1936, a markedly foggy day, two Handley Page Heyford bombers flying in company caused a stir when they unexpectedly began to circle in the vicinity of Disley, near Whaley Bridge, on the outskirts of Manchester, with yet more interest being generated when it was realised that they were probing the fog with the intention of actually setting down.

The first of the bombers, K4868, as it would transpire, the Heyford flown by Squadron Leader Charles Attwood, made its approach as the other, K6898, continued to circle. Squadron Leader Attwood chose a field of some length at The Homestead, on Jackson Edge, then the property of Mr R. Whitworth, touched down, and came to a halt, having landed safely. The other machine, flown, as the witnesses were to discover, by Pilot Officer Michael Clifford, then made an approach some two hundred yards off, only in the course of its landing run struck a telegraph pole and two fences before finishing up with its nose buried in Mr Whitworth's garden, its tail high in the air. Notwithstanding the upset, however, the crew emerged unscathed, if with one of them, the leading-aircraftman wireless operator, not a little shaken by having had a propeller blade slice through the thin metal wall of his station.

Heyford K6898 embedded in the garden of The Homestead at Disley

The unheralded arrival of these two monster aircraft, particularly in such poor weather, came as a surprise to the good people of Disley, but as both the local and the national newspapers would later inform them, the joint arrival told only part of a story. A story which had begun earlier that day when seven Handley Page Heyford bombers of No. 102 (Ceylon) Squadron, having completed a detachment to Ulster's RAF Aldergrove (to become Belfast International Airport), were detailed to return in formation to their home station of RAF Finningley, near Doncaster, in Yorkshire.

No. 102 Squadron, a unit on the strength of a Bomber Command newly metamorphosed from the bomber element of Air Defence of Great Britain (ADGB) Command, had itself only emerged from its sixteen years of post-First World War disbandment in October 1935, and had only begun operating independently since March 1936. When the time came to leave

Ulster the leader appointed was Squadron Leader Attwood. He would have been well aware that widespread fog and ice had led to chaotic conditions over much of the mainland, that only two days before, bad weather had contributed to the disastrous crash of an airliner near Croydon, and that snow had now moved in to exacerbate the situation. This conjunction of fog and heavy snowstorms: a steep pressure gradient combating a slacker one; would also have suggested significant wind changes. As it was, probably not in the least mindful of the squadron motto which translated as 'Attempt and Achieve', Squadron Leader Attwood briefed his seven crews.

His intention was to make a dog-leg of the flight. Initially, during the anticipated good weather phase of the route, he would aim for the shortest sea crossing, some 115 miles, with a landfall at Barrow. He would then steer directly for Finningley, 110 miles further on. A good proposal, particularly in view of the weather, with each pilot and observer (navigator) producing a flight plan for their own aircraft against the event that they became detached from the formation.

This had to be considered, for although the Heyford's stability made it a good machine for flying formation in, holding close station would have been unnecessarily stressful, therefore Squadron Leader Attwood settled upon a loose Vic disposition, with himself in the van.

By all accounts everything went well as far as the landfall. After that, however, the weather encountered seems to have been even worse than anticipated, and things began to go awry. What is clear, is that only Pilot Officer Clifford found it possible, or politic, perhaps, to maintain station with the leader. But that the other pilots could not, or chose not to, do so, would have been a matter of no great moment, for in their basic role as night bombers each crew was expected to be capable of operating independently.

So it was that, having found himself acting under his own auspices, Sergeant Pilot Biddulph followed his observer's directions, and not without some difficulty, landed at Finningley only a little behind the planned estimated time. Interviewed in the eighties by author Ron Collier he was able to describe how, on arrival, he initially thought he was the last one to arrive and expected, therefore, some ribbing at the very least. Only to find that he was the first, and for that day certainly, to be the only safe arrival. [Having landed safely, there was no requirement for Sergeant Biddulph to raise an incident report, consequently the registration of his aircraft remains to be determined.]

Flying Heyford K4864, Sergeant Pilot Williams had also distanced himself from the formation and flown on, but having let down in accordance with his observer's estimate, he had broken cloud to find that snow was now further reducing the fog-impaired visibility. At once, already aware that he was in severe icing conditions, he had decided upon making a precautionary landing, and seeing a suitable looking field, had set up his approach. He had touched down successfully enough, but, like Pilot Officer Clifford at Disley, he too had encountered a telegraph pole in the course of his landing run. This had slewed him off into a ploughed field, but although the aircraft was badly damaged, none of the crew was hurt. They discovered, however, that they had put down at Blyborough, in Lincolnshire, which meant that while their track keeping had been good they had overflown Finningley by some seventeen miles.

Flying Officer John Gyll-Murray (Flying Officer John Edwin Campbell Gascoigne Flemyng Gyll-Murray!), flying Heyford L5188, similarly made his way independently, but on letting down after the calculated lapse time and sighting the ground, found himself in the vicinity of York, the correct distance along track, but nearly thirty miles north of Finningley; a powerful indicator that a wind change had seriously upset his observer's calculations. Unphased by this he pragmatically picked out a suitable field, let down, and made a successful landing; almost certainly then, making a bee line for the nearest telephone.

The epic of Heyford K4874, abandoned by Flight Lieutenant Villiers and his crew, is told in *Derbyshire's High Peak Air Crash Sites, Northern Section,* page 136.

The crew of the final aircraft, K6900, were not as fortunate as any of the others. Piloted by Sergeant Victor Charles Otter, their aircraft too let down according to estimate, and emerged from the cloud rack, but into thick fog. Sergeant Otter at once levelled from his descent, and began to search out a landing site, only to fly into a steep hillside moments later.

Villagers a mile beyond Hebden Bridge, to the north-west of Halifax, who had heard the crash, hurried up the hill to lend assistance, but were hampered by the fog. When they eventually reached the scene it was to find that the aircraft had run on a hundred yards or so after striking but had then burst into flames and burnt out. Sergeant Otter was discovered to be alive, if injured, but the other three occupants had been killed: the observer, Sergeant D.G. Church; the fitter, Leading Aircraftman P.G Clements; and the wireless operator, Aircraftman C.V. Bodenham. One of these, although which one is unspecified in the contemporary reports, had attempted to abandon, for his body, together with his partially-streamed parachute, was found some way from the machine, suggesting that the aircraft, already heavy with ice, had been only marginally controllable and that an order to abandon might have been given. This aircraft too, was reasonably on track, but some forty miles short of Finningley.

Of the dispersed aircraft, Heyfords K4868 and K5188 were flown back to base the next day. Nevertheless this was a debacle of the first order, and a set back to the Royal Air Force in the process, as it was, of building up its bomber force – indeed, so great was the urgency of the build up that six replacement aircraft were delivered to the squadron just three days later, on 12 December 1936! It was a set back, however, from which lessons could be learned, and which spurred on the development of de-icing systems on large aircraft.

Nor did it unduly affect the future of some, at least, of those pilots concerned. Certainly, three of them survived the war, two achieving senior-officer status, Sergeant Biddulph rising to Squadron Leader, and Flight Lieutenant Villiers to Wing Commander. Sergeant Otter, however, rose even higher, for he was commissioned in 1941 and had reached squadron leader by 1945 when he transferred to the technical branch. Progressing in that branch he reached Group Captain rank in 1956, and was then translated to air rank, to Air Commodore in 1962 and to Air Vice Marshal in 1967. Not too bad for a lowly senior NCO pilot who, in 1936, could not even find his way from Ulster to Yorkshire.

The Heyfords' set-down area at Disley

VISITING THE SITE

There is no visual evidence of the Disley set-down, and virtually no local awareness of the incident, while The Homestead is a vastly altered and strictly private property. Its owner, however, Mrs Miranda Johnson, was able to advise that the photograph of the tail-high Heyford had long been displayed in one of the Disley pubs.

Chapel-en-le-Frith

36. Biplane, 1918
Lydgate Farm, Eccles Pike, near Chapel-en-le-Frith

SK 04056 81370 260 m
Unit and Station: RAF
Date: 3 December 1918
Crew: pilot, unknown

In her book, *Except the Lord Build the House*, Rose Hannah Swindells relates how, on 3 December 1918, as a schoolgirl at Bugsworth – now re-styled Buxworth –, an aeroplane came down in a field belonging to Lydgate Farm. She wrote, 'I did not see a Zeppelin high up in the air which happened to pass over Bugsworth, but I resolved to see an aeroplane and made my way

to where it was stranded, or more correctly, grounded. The light was fading. I was not very big and there was a thorny hedge bordering the field and ditch in front of it. I strode over the ditch and could just see over the hedge … to see the wing of the aircraft and pilot standing by it. He turned his head and looked at me and I looked at him, and then clambered back on the track and set off home.' Although the field was identified, nobody met to date has known anything more of the event.

The pilot looked at me

Looking into the field below Eccles Pike where the unknown biplane set down

VISITING THE SITE

Mrs Swindells gave a detailed description of the route she took to the set-down, halfway up the slopes of Eccles Pike, 'crossing Goodman's New Road' [Back Eccles Lane] 'and following a cart track' [by 2013, long redundant, the public footpath having been re-routed]. Nothing to see, but the Eccles Pike summit, even scaled from the road, is well worthwhile.

37. Miles Magister Mk.1 L6908
Chapel-en-le-Frith High School grounds

SK 05313 30224 242 m
Unit and Station: No. 16 Elementary Flying Training School,
RAF Burnaston, Derby, No. 51 Group, Flying Training Command
Date: 27 August 1941
Crew: pilot, slightly injured
• Leading Aircraftman Muirhead, pupil pilot

On 27 August 1943 pupil-pilot Leading Aircraftman Muirhead, having logged twenty-three hours solo on the Magister, was dispatched from RAF Burnaston on a general-handling detail built around practising steep turns. Having lost himself, he attempted a precautionary landing at what was then Marsh Green Farm, Chapel-en-le-Frith, some thirty miles from Burnaston, but hit a tree and crashed. The machine was taken away by a Queen Mary low loader.

The Magister's impact point, now landscaped over

VISITING THE SITE

The line of trees the aircraft hit was still extant in 2013, but the terminal impact site had long since been landscaped to form a shrubbery between the railway embankment and the High School car park.

38. Airspeed Oxford Mk.1 V3210
Chapel-en-le-Frith

No more exact location established by early 2014

Unit and Station: RAF College Cranwell, Lincolnshire, No. 21 Group, Flying Training Command

Date: 2 September 1941

Crew: one injured.

• Pilot, Leading Aircraftman B.C. Forsdick, injured

On 2 September 1941 pupil pilot Leading Aircraftman B.C. Forsdick was detailed to carry out a solo cross-country flight in Oxford V3210. Just after mid-day, having encountered cloudy conditions and with fog masking the terrain, he struck high ground, and was injured. The investigation criticised him for entering cloud, and the unit's navigation instructor for not having checked the route details.

The summary of the RAF crash report, the handwritten Form 1180, has the crash occurring at (the non-existent) *Consburn Moor*, Chapel-en-le-Frith. Having it in mind that in a similar report the location verbally passed as 'Moorwood' was recorded as Maud, locations such as the Cowburn Tunnel beneath Colborne Moor (2 miles north-east) were investigated. To date, however, neither local canvassing nor press appeals have resulted in an identification of this site.

Crash report summary (F1180) for Oxford V3201, Chapel-en-le-Frith

39. Unidentified trainer
Lower Crossings, Chapel-en-le-Frith

SK 05141 80301 232 m
Unit and Station: Unknown
Date: 1942
Crew: pilot, slightly injured
• Charles Bowen, RAF Volunteer Reserve

Mr Ron Lomas, of Chapel-en-le-Frith, witnessed this accident. 'At the time,' he explained, 'I was working at Crossings Garage at the junction of the old A6 and the Crossings Road [SK 04995 80457] – it's a tarmac company now. The pilot was a Charlie Bowen from one of the big houses that were then spaced along the road. As the plane came towards us it hit one of a line of trees some fields back from the road, and crashed. I picked up a fire extinguisher and started running, but crossing the first drystone wall I dropped the extinguisher and it discharged. So I ran on, over what was a marshy patch, then over another wall, to find the plane not badly damaged, although Mr Bowen had a cut nose. And that was it, really. I just went back to work.'

The tree line at Lower Crossings

VISITING THE SITE

The site is some 200 yards into the housing estate from the road, while the tree line has become the boundary between Chapel-en-le-Frith High School and the estate.

40. De Havilland DH82A Tiger Moth
Rushup Farm, Sparrowpit

SK 09351 81188 346 m
Unit and Station: No. 19 Elementary Flying Training School,
RAF Sealand (Chester), Flying Training Command
Date: c.1941
Crew: pupil pilot, unhurt
- Identity unknown

When a Sealand-based Tiger Moth, lost in mist, put down at Rushup Farm, Sparrowpit, the pupil pilot spent a cosseted night at the farm. Next morning a sergeant flying instructor recovered pupil and machine, performing aerobatics for farmer Mr Alan Virtue and his wife before setting course. Not a crash, but a precautionary landing recalling the advisory in the contemporary *RAF Elementary Flying Manual*: Pay for hospitality. Country folk are often poor as well as generous.

The Tiger Moth set-down at Sparrowpit

VISITING THE SITE

The field, long since divided by a crosswise fence, is beside the Sparrowpit-Castleton road, so can be viewed from the car!

41. Avro, 1919
Sparrowpit

Date: 15 January 1919

Enthusiast sources record that an Avro biplane came down near Sparrowpit on 15 January 1919, but nothing more was discovered. For posterity then.

Buxton Area

42. Avro Anson Mk.1 L7968
Moss House Farm, Combs Moss, north-west of Buxton

SK 04615 75097 446 m
Unit and Station: Central Navigation School, RAF Cranage,
No. 25 Group, Flying Training Command
Date: 15 October 1942
Crew: four, all killed

- Sergeant Paul Joseph Woodcock, RAF Volunteer Reserve, staff pilot
- Sergeant Richard James Reay, Royal Canadian Air Force, pilot
- Sergeant James Munro Matheson, RCAF, pilot
- Sergeant William Gordon Dale, RAFVR,
  staff wireless operator/air gunner

On 15 October 1942 Sergeant Paul Woodcock, a staff pilot at the Central Navigation School, supported by his staff wireless operator, was detailed to fly a night navigational exercise with two Canadian pilot-pupils. At 2215 hours, however, while homing towards Cranage, he clipped the top of a ridge to the north-west of Buxton and sixteen miles from base. All four occupants were killed.

The court of inquiry submitted that the crew must have let down early, having mistaken the Cranage occulting beacon for the Cranage pundit beacon, a deduction based upon the fact that no request was made for a course to steer. Senior Authority concurred, directing that all No. 25 Group aircrews were made aware of the difference between occults and pundits.

Yet the conclusion supposes that the fliers had based their estimate of distance-to-go upon a light! – whether occult or pundit. Direction, of course, but hardly range: even though there were (theoretical) ranges associated with each. The most likely scenario, then, is that the crew relaxed when they saw an identifying light and without taking the basic precaution of double-checking their position, complacently let down over a blacked-out land and into high ground. As so many had done before them, and so many more were still to do.

Terminal site of Anson L7968, looking towards Moss House Farm

Moss Bank debris

VISITING THE SITE

The Moss House Farm track (at SK 04594 74344), with opportunity parking on the A5004, gives access to the very fine Moss Bank ridge and beyond, although the impact site bears no scars and only metal-detected debris has been found in recent years.

43. Boulton-Paul Defiant T3921
Shining Tor, near Cat and Fiddle Inn, Buxton

SJ 99906 73401 506 m

Unit and Station: No. 96 Squadron, RAF Cranage, Cheshire,
No. 9 Group, Fighter Command

Date: 16 October 1941

Crew: two, both injured

- Pilot Officer M.G. Hilton, pilot
- Sergeant H.W. Brunckhorst, air gunner

Having completed a liaison exercise with a controlling radar station, the crew of Defiant T3921 began a descent towards Cranage. Pilot Officer Hilton had even lowered the undercarriage for landing. But the aircraft was still fourteen miles from Cranage when it was flown into the eastern side of Shining Tor. It was wrecked on impact, but did not burn, and both men survived to fly again.

The inquiry ascertained, that, being in cloud as he descended through 2,500 feet, Pilot Officer Hilton had been concentrating on instrument flying, and had been unaware that he had emerged from cloud, or that he was still over high ground.

Crash site of Defiant T3921, from abeam the path to Shining Tor,
looking towards Tors Ridge

VISITING THE SITE

This is the lowest of the three crash sites on the slope immediately below Shining Tor. There is parking opposite the Cat and Fiddle Inn, and rather less where the Errwood track leaves the A543 (SK 00006 72126, 500 m). After 0.72 miles – 20 minutes – along the Errwood track, turning left towards Shining Tor and descending for 300 yards (to SJ 99859 73358, 507 m, where well-maintained field wall and path-side wall meet) leaves the site 210 feet away, off path, on 040°M. (In 2013 the site was shared with a ruinous shooting butt No.8.)

The co-ordinates are those logged by Mr Phil Shaw in 1970 (a former ranger and 33 years in the Mountain-Rescue Service yet, by choice, he walks barefooted!) In the seventies, he remembers, when he and Ron Collier visited, there was very little debris left. Certainly, nothing has been found recently.

Being already off path, the Norseman and Harvard sites (Part One, Sections 16 and 17) are as easily visited by continuing to warily heather bash. The Norseman site is 210 yards upslope on 340°M (in 2013, beyond a No.5 shooting butt), the Harvard a further 200 yards on 339°M. Shining Tor, with its must-linger-at viewpoint (not forgetting the ridge path, with an end to heather and bilberry!), is then another 300 yards directly upslope on 270°M.

44. Auster Autocrat G-ALUE
Axe Edge Moor, near Buxton

SK 02224 70424 480 m
Owner: Private ownership
Date: 20 September 1952
Occupants: two, pilot and passenger, unhurt
- Mr Kenneth Stockfis, pilot
- Mr Charles Kitchen, passenger

When non-radio-equipped Auster Autocrat G-ALUE was inadvertently flown into Axe Edge Moor in low cloud in September 1952, its pilot, Mr Kenneth Stockfis, knew that no immediate search-and-rescue operation would be launched.

He and his passenger, Mr Charles Kitchen, had already been fortunate in coming down on a relatively level area of moorland, for cloud-mantled ridges reared two hundred feet above them. They were even more fortunate in having found themselves uninjured when they had scrambled from their inverted and badly-damaged aircraft. So, shocked and disorientated, with the fog drastically reducing visibility and the evening light fading, Mr Stockfis made the always problematical decision to leave the wreck and set off to seek help.

Unaware that they were less than half a mile from the main Buxton to Congleton road, they began ploughing their way in the opposite direction, further into the moor. Just the same, their relative good fortune held, for when Mr Kitchen found himself floundering, soaking wet, in a bog, they turned back to the relative shelter – and the more easily located bulk – of the wreck.

They then endured a long and uncomfortable night, only to find, as dawn broke, that the fog was even thicker. Upon which, deciding that there was still slim chance of anyone happening upon them, they set out to seek succour once again. Yet they again headed south-westwards, away from the nearby roads, and therefore, further into the moor. Fortune, however, continued to mellow towards them, for eventually they stumbled into the remote holding of Orchard Farm, one-and-a-half hard moorland miles from the crash site. Here they found hot drinks, and food, but no telephone, although before long the news was carried to the local policeman at Quarnford, Constable Frank Gardner. His daughter, Brenda, later to become Mrs Farlam, of Wallnook Farm, Brand Side, remembered that summons.

'I would often accompany Dad on call-outs, indeed, he'd have me take down the details in shorthand. So we biked over to Orchard Farm – no car in those days, of course – to find that Joe and Lizzie Wardle had taken good care of the two men. Then, in company with Mr Edwards, an Automobile Association patrolman, we set off over Bareleg and Cheeks-Hill to keep an eye on the aircraft. It was smashed, and I don't suppose it was much use. But I can't remember what happened to it after Dad passed over the responsibility.'

Farmer John Bowler, though, of Tor Gate Farm, Wildboarclough, remembered the Auster with gratitude. For safety, its fuel tank had to be emptied of its relatively low-octane contents. And, serendipitously, his motor-bike, parked on Thatch Marsh Lane, only 300 yards distant, had a tank with plenty of spare capacity.

In fact, the Auster was subsequently recovered from the moor, after which, rebuilt and re-registered, it flew happily on at Barton for several years until it was eventually destroyed in a mid-air collision.

The area in which Auster G-ALUE came down

VISITING THE SITE

There is no visible sign of the crash, and not the least incentive in tramping that particular bit of heather.

45. Supermarine Spitfire Mk.2A P7560
Thirkelow Farm, near Harpur Hill, Buxton

SK 04975 68961 430 m

Unit and Squadron: No. 131 Squadron, RAF Atcham, Shrewsbury, No. 9 Group, Fighter Command.

Date: 22 November 1941

Crew: pilot, parachuted safely

- Flight Sergeant Briggs, Royal Australian Air Force

On 22 November 1941 newly-joined squadron member Flight Sergeant Briggs was to carry out a practice fighter sweep – basically a navigational exercise – in order to build up his operational experience. As he moved over high ground, however, he found cloud closing about him. Having had very little experience in flying on instruments, he called to ask whether he should abort the exercise or carry on. Receiving no answer – it would be deduced later that his radio had failed – he decided to carry on. Just minutes later, though, seeing a hill looming, he was forced to power up and pull back. Only to enter even thicker cloud, become disorientated, and lose control.

He knew that he had scant time to spend in attempting to regain control. So using a degree of judgement hardly to be expected of his skimpy 140 hours, he pushed back his hood, and baled out. That he landed within a few hundred yards of his aircraft showed just how wise he had been!

Flight Sergeant Harris parachuted into this field. The farm is to the left

The abandoned aircraft, the full-power crescendo of its engine warning of its approach, plunged into the yard of Thirkelow Farm and caught fire, one wing slicing through the roof of a substantial stone barn into which three boys, playing in the yard only seconds before, had hastily taken shelter.

Thirkelow Barn, Mr John Swain is standing on the impact point. One wing sliced through the roof tiles but the three sheltering boys were unhurt

The investigation found inexperience to be the main cause, although the failed radio took some blame, the squadron's commanding officer penning, 'lack of airmanship in deciding to continue on course when R/T had failed'. Just the same, no further action was taken.

The wreck was quickly cleared, but evidently some debris was overlooked, for when Mr John Swain took up residence some aircraft-derived aluminium members still lingered in a corner of the damaged barn. Then, many years later, while lowering the surface of the yard itself, he discovered the blue, verdigris-like corrosion so indicative of an aircraft crash site. The roof of the damaged barn, however, which for many years had shown the mismatch where the original grey-stone tiles had been replaced with blue slates, he later re-roofed, incorporating the tiles into the farm proper, after which no trace of the Spitfire crash remained.

What Mr Swain still possessed, however, was a set of cobweb-covered pilot's goggles found in the barn.

Flying goggles, top, 1950s issue and bottom, from the 1940s

VISITING THE SITE

Footpaths thread the area, while the farm can be accessed from the Leap Edge road, but there is nothing to see, and it is private property.

46. Miles Master Mk.3 W8455
King Sterndale, south-east of Buxton

SK 09625 71497 247 m

Unit and Squadron: No. 5 (Pilots) Advanced Flying Unit, RAF Ternhill, near Market Drayton, No. 21 Group, Flying Training Command

Date: 12 October, 1942

Crew: pilot, survived

- Sergeant F.J. Flower

The relatively high performance Miles Master ate up ground very swiftly, accordingly, when pupil-pilot Sergeant Flower was dispatched on a general map-reading exercise from the Advanced Flying Training Unit at RAF Ternhill, near Market Drayton, Shropshire, he was briefed to remain within fifteen miles of the airfield. Yet two hours after getting airborne, finding himself hopelessly lost, and with his fuel tanks virtually dry, he set about making a precautionary landing to the south-east of Buxton, and some forty miles adrift.

Farmer Joe Lomas, of King Sterndale, whose land Sergeant Flower selected, was able to piece together the actual touchdown. 'He came from the south-east,' he said, 'just cleared the gorge of Deep Dale, and landed uphill on our Footpath Field. It was a relatively smooth grass field – and there were no power cables then – but he obviously struck quite hard and bounced, for wherever he had touched the ground the propeller had churned out great grooves. Then the wingtips broke off, followed by the tail, and just before the plane stopped, the engine – it was one of the big radials.' He pondered. 'When dad and I got there the RAF still hadn't arrived, but a succession of villagers came to look. Though I never did see the pilot.'

Miss Freda Hamilton, of nearby Cowdale, however, was able to account for that. 'No, for our vicar, the Reverend Robert Main and his wife, were among the first on the scene and took him home to the Vicarage and fed him tea until the authorities collected him.'

Sergeant Flower's commanding officer was far less accommodating, for while taking into account the bad visibility, and the little experience the student had – under two-hundred hours total flying, and only five hours on Masters – he had the sergeant's flying log book endorsed, 'Carelessness and disobedience'. The Ternhill station commander was even harsher, fulminating, 'A stupid, careless, error of judgement'.

For all that, the forced landing itself had not been too badly done, for the sergeant had touched down a sensible distance up the field. Albeit that things had, quite literally, come to pieces rather after that, the rising ground causing him to underestimate the degree of nose-up round out required.

The set-down site

VISITING THE SITE

Parking is plentiful, but there is nothing to be seen at the site, for as Mr Lomas explained, 'The RAF dragged the wreckage up to the road and took it off on a low-loader. They had to take down a few walls, which they then rebuilt. But they didn't leave anything. And although the marks the propeller made were visible for years afterwards they've long been ploughed out.'

47. Pierre Robin R1180TD G-CRAN
Staden Industrial Estate, Buxton

SK 07044 72118 333 m

Operator: Private aircraft, Tatenhill, Needwood

Date: 15 June 1996

Occupants: four, all killed

- Mr Joe Smith, pilot
- Miss Mary Jane Smith, aged 11
- Miss Joanne Smith, aged 12
- Miss Elizabeth Skupien, aged 11

Robin

On 15 June 1996 entrepreneur Mr Joe Smith took off from Tatenhill Airfield, near Needwood, in Robin G-CRAN on a pleasure trip to mark his daughter, Mary Jane's, eleventh birthday. His other passengers were Joanne, his twelve-year old, and Elizabeth Skupien, the girls' friend. On reaching the Buxton area, however, the aircraft was stalled, and crashed, killing all on board.

Mr Smith's route, flown at between 500 and 1,000 feet, had taken in Alton Towers, Riber Castle, and the stone circle at Arbour Low. He had then set course towards Slade Farm, to the south of Buxton, the home of the Brittain family, where his daughters had spent the previous evening.

Mr John Brittain was serving a customer in the farm shop when the Robin came into sight. 'I was intent on what I was doing,' he remembered, 'and even when it waggled its wings I didn't associate it with the birthday flight. Indeed, when there was a loud bang I jokingly said to my customer, "I wonder if that aeroplane's crashed?" "I shouldn't think so," she smiled, and we carried on with the transaction.

His grandson, Phillip Brittain-Cartlidge, however, had been left with no such ease of mind. 'I knew whose plane it was at once,' he recalled, 'and I waved to them as they passed. Mr Smith was waggling his wings, going slowly, with his flaps down. Then he turned away towards Slade House and the ridge. And suddenly the engine misfired!' He paused. 'I saw the nose dip down and the plane begin to descend even lower. But then it passed out of my line of sight towards the ridge. And I began to run.'

Other witnesses from the nearby industrial estate told the coroner's court that when the engine misfired the pilot had turned to line up with one of the service roads and seemed all set to make a forced-landing; that at an estimated one hundred feet above the ground, when the engine had picked up again, they had seen the nose lift sharply. And finally they described how the nose-high aircraft staggered, then fell off into a steeply nose-down spiral to the left to impact heavily with the ground.

The crashed Robin

Phillip Brittain-Cartlidge reached the aircraft in a matter of moments, as he related. 'When I got there two men from City Electrical Factors were already there. There was no fire, but the perspex canopy had gone, leaving the cockpit open to view, and it was only too obvious that nothing could be done.' Again he paused. 'It was only later that the full trauma of it came home to me.'

Phillip's mother, Mrs Elizabeth Brittain-Cartlidge, touched on the trauma too. 'For quite a time we wondered if we'd distracted them by waving. And what made it so much worse was that just before we parted the night before, Mary Jane had whispered that she had something to tell me. It was late, though, and her mother was calling, so I put her off, "Tell me tomorrow, dear," I told her.'

One of the ironies was that the tragedy occurred during the 1996 firemen's strike, so that four RAF support vehicles and an army Green Goddess fire engine arrived in answer to the emergency call. 'Regrettably there was not a lot to be done at the scene,' the secretary of the striking Derbyshire Fire Brigade Union was quoted as saying.

The official inquiry ascertained that Mr Smith had held a Private Pilot's Licence for several years, logging 865 hours, if only four on the Robin. There had been no need for him to maintain radio contact, so, poignantly, photographs the girls had taken were used to recreate his route.

The investigators carried out an exhaustive examination of the engine but were unable to reproduce the symptoms reported by witnesses. They found, therefore, that the aircraft had been asked to climb with such suddenness that it had stalled and fallen into an incipient spin, then nosed into the ground.

The Robin impact site, long since built over

VISITING THE SITE

Industrial buildings have long covered the site, but in an endearing touch, the side garden of nearby Slade Farm has been planted with daffodils which, in springtime, blossom to form the initial letters of each girl's name: *Rough winds*, indeed, *do shake the darling buds* ...

48. Avro Biplane, 1919
Colt Croft Farm, Buxton

SK 06885 72310 325 m

Date: 15 January 1919

Various enthusiast sources, some using the above date, have a biplane coming down at Colt Croft Farm, on Duke's Drive, Buxton. No local awareness could be found, so the incident is recorded for posterity.

Wildboarclough

49. Avro Anson Mk.1 N9858
Dane Bower, Wildboarclough

SK 00311 69926 501 m

Unit and Squadron: No. 10 Flying Training School, RAF Ternhill,
south-west of Market Drayton, Stoke-on-Trent,
No. 21 Group, Flying Training Command

Date: 14 November, 1940

Crew: pupil pilot, killed

- Leading Aircraftman Martin James Walton Taylor

Anson N9858, Dane Bower, looking towards Shutlingsloe

On 14 November 1940, when pupil pilot Leading Aircraftman Martin Taylor was dispatched in Anson N9858 on a navigation test, he was relatively advanced in his pilot training, having logged 109 hours total flying, with twenty-two dual and thirty-six hours solo on the Anson. He got himself lost, however, strayed into an area of high ground in bad visibility, and died when he flew into Dane Bower at 1,600 feet above sea level.

The court of inquiry noted that the weather on the correct route had remained perfectly suitable for the exercise. As for getting lost, they looked, among other things, at the possibility that this inexperienced pilot had incorrectly set his directional gyroscope – basically a dead-beat compass repeater. They would also have had to consider spatial disorientation leading to loss of control in poor visibility. But with so many sources of error to choose from, they finally had to submit that they were unable to attribute the accident to anything but faulty navigation, which in turn, had to stem from inexperience.

VISITING THE SITE

The crash site lies 600 yards up a farmland track – now private – off the A54. The track would have made the recovery straightforward, so nothing is to be seen, although scraps have been found.

50. Airspeed Oxford Mk.1 LX673
Dingers Hollow Farm, north of Wildboarclough

SJ 98076 70876 387 m impact point

SJ 98142 70919 352 m debris pool

Unit and Squadron: No. 21 (Pilots) Advanced Flying Unit,
RAF Wheaton Aston, Stafford, No. 21 Group, Flying Training Command

Date: 11 January 1946

Crew: two, both killed

- Flying Officer David Fairless Oliver, RAF Volunteer Reserve, staff pilot
- Flight Sergeant Eric Bulcock, RAFVR, pupil pilot

On 11 January 1946 staff instructor Flying Officer David Oliver took off with his pupil, Flight Sergeant Eric Bulcock, to practise Standard Beam Approaches (SBA). A mistake was made, however, and the pupil was allowed to come 'too low on the back beam', as the RAF accident report recorded. Both pilots died as the aircraft struck a gully above Dingers Hollow Farm, just north of Wildboarclough.

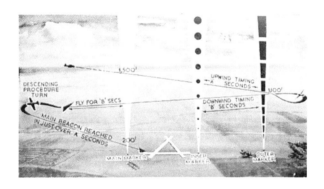

Back Beam Approach

It was very easy for even an experienced pilot to become confused when flying an SBA pattern. This was especially the case when making a 'back-beam' approach, for the back beam – as opposed to the normally-used front beam – had no range-marker beacons. This meant that a relatively complicated timing procedure was called for in order to determine how long to head away from the airfield before turning back and beginning the landing approach. Yet as the RAF's 1941 *Air Navigation* manual warned, 'mathematical ability is one of the first faculties … to suffer in flight'. Even so, the inquiry was unable to fathom why the timing had been so grossly inaccurate as to take the aircraft so far beyond any safety zone and into hilly ground.

There were two witnesses to the tragedy, Mr John Finney, of High Ash Farm, and Mr W. Hoggarth of Dry Knowle Farm. They heard a low-flying aircraft droning through the thick mist and heavy rain. Then the twin-engined trainer emerged from the mist. They saw it strike the top of the hill, and one of its wings detach. After which it reared nose up, only to fall backwards down the slope and into the gully, breaking up as it went.

The Dingers Hollow debris-spill area. The impact site is to the top right

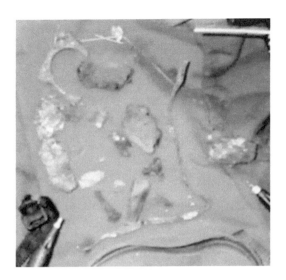

Oxford debris

VISITING THE SITE

Parking is available on the Bottom-of-the-Oven to Wildboarclough road at SJ 98426 70578, some 500 yards from Dingers Hollow Farm. Having obtained permission to enter the land, the terminal site is some 170 yards upslope. Metal-detector searches still reveal corroded scraps, but to find surface evidence is rare.

51. Airspeed Oxford Mk.1 L4601
Shutlingsloe, Wildboarclough

SJ 97639 69347 431 m
Unit and Squadron: No. 17 Service Flying Training School,
RAF Cranwell, Sleaford, Lincolnshire,
No. 21 Group, Flying Training Command
Date: 4 April 1945
Occupants: five, two passengers and one pilot killed; the aircraft captain
and a passenger injured
- Flying Officer Horace Keith Shawyer, pilot, instructor, injured
- Flight Lieutenant Horace Garth Featonby, pilot under training, killed
- Corporal A.J. Burd, passenger, injured
- Leading Aircraftman Frederick Roscoe, passenger, killed
- Aircraftman First Class George Fishwick, passenger, killed

On 4 April 1945 Flying Officer Horace Shawyer, a staff instructor, was detailed to supervise a pupil pilot on a daytime navigational cross-country exercise. Three off-duty airmen went along for the ride.

After forty-five minutes, however, Flying Officer Shawyer found himself faced with lowering cloud. Aware of the hilly terrain ahead but reluctant, perhaps, to upset his pupil's navigational timing, he did not order a climb. As a result, when the cloud thickened, the aircraft was flown into the southern shoulder of Shutlingsloe. There was no fire, but the impact killed Flight Lieutenant Horace Featonby, Leading-Aircraftman Frederick Roscoe, and Aircraftman First Class George Fishwick. Flying Officer Shawyer and Corporal Burd, were injured.

The inquiry held that Flying Officer Shawyer should have climbed to a safe height on encountering cloud and not tried to fly below it. In view of this, a summary of evidence – the normal precursor to a court martial – was ordered to be held once the instructor was deemed well enough to appear. What the outcome of the summary was, however, is not known.

Mr Phillip Sharpley, who was brought up at the nearby Crag Inn, remembered that his fourteen-year-old brother, Frank, was alone at home when the police arrived in search of a vehicle that could bring down the casualties. 'Frank told them,' he recalled, 'that he could drive our 1937 Fordson up there with a trailer, except that this would mean temporarily leaving the farm tracks. Even so, they urged him to get under way. So he duly brought back three bodies. At which the police told him they'd now prosecute him for driving on public road … Though they were probably joking.'

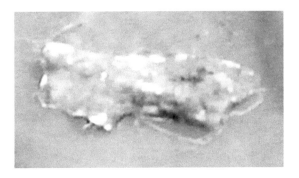

The sole fragment found

VISITING THE SITE

Ample parking is available at Clough House (SJ 98713 69888), just north of Wildboarclough. A footpath then leads towards Shutlingsloe – a well worthwhile ascent! To access the site, however, turning from the path at SJ 97739 69436 on a heading of 223°M, leaves just 150 yards of rough going. But there is nothing to be seen, though the only sizeable boulder marks the impact area.

These are incidents which appear on enthusiast lists on websites, in books, and in popular lore, but which investigation has either shown to have no substance, or conversely, substance enough to keep on record for future research.

German bomber, Little London Road, Sheffield,

A persistent tale, which has made it into print, has it that a German bomber, hit by anti-aircraft fire, fell in pieces in the vicinity of Stoke's paint factory in Little London Road. Mr Stokes, the managing director of the company, remembered his father, Mr J.B.W. Stokes, refuting this tale. It started, it seems, after two of a stick of bombs hit the factory, one igniting the white-spirit store, the other burning out the company's stock of labels. Mr Stoke, senior, however, always spoke benignly of the bombing, maintaining, 'It was our best advert. Those labels which didn't ignite, were blasted up and drifted all over Nether Edge!' A spurious report then, as a bomber crash-site, but possibly something for the urban walker, unable to get to the moors, to smile over.

RAF Type, Coal Aston crash

On 20 January 1919 the *Sheffield Daily Telegraph* reported the funeral of Sergeant Pilot A.W. Ellis, of Sheffield, recording that it was attended by 'two other sergeant pilots from Coal Aston'. Some enthusiast sources tender this as a Coal Aston crash. In fact, the fatal accident occurred in Dublin.

Lysander V9577, Whaley Bridge

Though featuring in an otherwise-reliable enthusiast's list, no substance was found. Moreover, Lysander V9577 is authoritatively recorded in the *Air Britain* series as having enjoyed an accident-free record. Another item, then, for completeness and posterity.

Avro Lancaster, Townend Farm
SK 07502 73999 333 m.

This incident appeared on an enthusiast's list which correctly recorded some relatively obscure locations. In this instance, however, no supporting evidence was found. Indeed, even the Groom family, who owned Townend Farm from 1952, repudiated the report. It is included here, therefore, to obviate fruitless searches.

Heinkel He111, Buxton Area, 'above Burbage'
Luftwaffe
Date: 17 March 1942
Crew: four, two names recorded
- *Hauptmann* Ernst Fraden
- *Leutnant* Frishau

Author Ron Collier listed this incident for a projected White Peaks crash-site book, noting that a Heinkel He111 ('one-eleven') came down 'above Burbage' on 17 March 1942; that two members of its crew, *Leutnant* [pilot officer] Frishau, and *Hauptmann* [flight lieutenant] Ernst Fraden were taken into custody by personnel from No. 28 Maintenance Unit of RAF Harpur Hill. So many specifics suggest that there is substance in the report so it recorded here against future research.

Junkers Ju88, Location unknown
Luftwaffe No. 106 *Kampfgeschwader* (KG 106: No. 106 Bomber Group)
Date: 3 July 1942
Crew: four, two surnames names recorded
- Bergman
- Majer

As with the previous entry, author Mr Ron Collier might have expanded upon the incident had ill-health not intervened. Again, it is hoped that the details might drive future research.

Airco Biplane
Peacock Hill, Baslow, near Chatsworth

SK 25705 72054
Unit and Station: RAF
Date: c. 1916
Crew: up to two

Interwing strut section showing the Airco insignia

As a young boy, Charles Roose, former chief clerk of the Chatsworth Estate, was told by a Baslow couple – Alf and Florrie Walker – of a First World War military biplane crashing below the Peacock Hotel at Baslow. Alf Walker was an Irish labourer who had helped construct the 28-mile long Derwent Valley Aqueduct from the upper, holding dams to pass under Chatsworth Park to Ambergate to supply water to Derby and Leicester.

Knowing of the youthful Charles' interest in aviation the couple gave him an interwing strut from the machine. Eventually Charles presented this to Eric Marsh of the Cavendish Hotel (Renamed from the Peacock in 1975) where it was still on display in 2014. Publication date for this book pressed before the type could be positively identified, but the strut bears the insignia of Airco, the company for which Geoffrey de Havilland produced such machines as the 1915 single-seater Airco DH2 pusher (defeater of the Fokker Scourge) and the highly successful DH9A bomber of 1918.

Mr Marsh, the owner of the strut, is a celebrated aviator and builder of several aircraft, some of which he has flown off the field where the Airco is held to have come down. In 2013, at the age of seventy, he began learning to fly a helicopter.

Crash location

Avro 504K G-EBJE
Pottery Area, Belper

SK 36331 47810 93m

Operator: Southern Counties Aviation Co. Ltd

Date: 11 October 1924

Occupants: pilot and four passengers. Pilot slightly injured

A cow observes the crashed Avro.

The biplane tourer was scheduled to remain in the Belper area for two weeks giving five-shilling joy rides. Having successfully carried his first load of four passengers the pilot topped up with locally purchased petrol. On the next take-off, as the Avro passed through fifty feet, the engine stopped, and the aircraft fell into the Pottery area of Belper – that containing the Glow Worm (now Vaillant) works and Pottery Primary School. The pilot injured his foot but his passengers were uninjured, as the *Derby Mercury* had it, 'really an extraordinary escape'. The paper included this 'flashlight' photo – featuring the cow –, while the text describes the damage: 'The nose of the machine was buried in the ground, the propeller broken to fragments and the undercarriage forced through the lower wing.'

The aircraft flew again from 1926 until 1934 when it was withdrawn from the civil register. It got airborne once more in June 1966 and moved to the RAF Museum in 1972 where, by 2013, its fuselage was married with the wings of Avro 548A G-EBKN.

Armstrong Whitworth Meteors NF.12 WS621, WS683
West Broughton Hollow and Sudbury Park Farm

Associated sites

Armstrong Whitworth Meteors NF.12 WS621, WS683

Attacking aircraft WS683, Sudbury Park Farm area, **SK 16460 33700** 93m

Target aircraft WS621, West Broughton Hollow, **SK 14602 33080** 89m

WS683, navigator, in tree, Alkmonton Bottoms, **SK 19320 38400** 115m

WS683, pilot's parachute, **SK 19198 38527** 131m

WS621, pilot's body, Dell Hole, **SK 14997 33071** 61m

Débris, Old Myers Farm, **SK 19010 35160** 90m

but also widely over Sudbury Prison and Park.

Unit and Station: No. 81 Group, Fighter Command,
All Weather Operational Conversion Unit, RAF North Luffenham.

Date: 21 September 1955

Crews: four, manually abandoned by parachute, one killed, three survived

- Pilot Officer Michael Aubrey Leslie Longman, killed, pilot WS621
- Pilot Officer David Harrington, navigator of WS 621, landed Sudbury Park Farm
- Pilot Officer Anthony (Tony) John Gladwell, pilot WS683, landed Alkmonton
- Pilot Officer Brian Bayley, navigator of WS683, landed Alkmonton

While night-exercising at 20,000 feet, Meteor WS683 commenced an inter-ception on WS621, but ended up colliding with the target.

When I researched this tragedy for my 2005 book, *The Peakland Air Crashes, The South* (the defunct Landmark Publishing), I had Pilot Officer Gladwell and his nav diving, Biggles-like, onto WS621 at high speed. Even in 2013, reprising my account for *White Peak Air Crash Sites* (Amberley Publishing), I had them approaching in a diving turn.

Later in 2013 former Pilot Officer Tony Gladwell contacted me and, accepting me as a non-warrior, transport-flier, was able to set me right about night-interception tactics at that time. He was also able to supply the names of both navigators, now given above, and to advise that the Meteors concerned were Armstrong Whitworth Night-Fighter Mark Twelves (NF.12s).

Mr Gladwell explained that the pilot had to get visual confirmation that the target was, indeed, a hostile before opening fire, that the NF12's elongated, radar-packed nose restricted the downwards view – ruling out diving attacks – so that interceptions were made from astern of the target, from slightly below it, and at a steadily-closing relative speed.

He remembered very vividly the sequence of events in his aircraft. His navigator, Pilot Officer Brian Bayley, had called, in quick succession, 'Range one thousand feet – Radar failure!' and then the imperative, 'Break starboard.'

Pilot Officer Gladwell had immediately rolled right to commence a maximum-rate turn away from their quarry, but even as he commenced to pull, had felt a slight jolt and advised, 'We've hit the target.' Realising that his aircraft was no longer answering to control – it had lost its tailplane – he initiated evacuation by pulling the hood-jettison handle. The hood, however, had been damaged by the impact and snagged him on exit, that and hypoxia, rendering him unconscious. Coming to in free fall, he pulled his ripcord and as his canopy opened, saw Pilot Officer Bayley descending nearby.

Pilot Officer Gladwell landed safely in a field of sleeping cows, at Alkmonton. Having collected himself, he found that Pilot Officer Bayley had landed in a tree and although unhurt, needed assistance from the fire service to get him down. Their aircraft crashed and burnt at Sudbury Park Farm, three miles to the south.

The crew of the target Meteor, WS621, caught totally unawares, baled out late. Pilot Officer David Harrington, the navigator, did so successfully. The pilot, however, Pilot Officer Michael Longman, had his parachute snag on the tailplane before tearing free to deposit him 400 yards beyond his aircraft, which crashed and burnt out at West Broughton Hollow.

The inquiry found the untimely-faulty radar to have been the main cause but recommended that a positioning constraint be introduced on some night practice interceptions.

The Jeffrey sisters, of Home Farm, West Broughton, heard WS621 crash. 'I thought it was thunder,' Mary recalls, 'then saw that our cabbage field was an inferno.' Her sister, Kate, remembered, 'Several lorry drivers had stopped this side of the field on what was then the main Uttoxeter Road. They could see parachute material wrapped around the tail, but the fire was too fierce for anyone to get near. And it had sliced through power cables, so they were a hazard too. And left the whole area without power for a day or so.'

Certainly, it was some time before the body of Pilot Officer Longman was found, in a tree, in nearby Dell Hole, now just across the A50 Trunk Road.

But as fire appliances began to arrive at West Broughton Hollow, reports were received of another jet skimming HM Prison, Sudbury, and exploding in a field at Sudbury Park Farm. Mr Wilf Carr, the farm manager, was returning from a fruitless search for this aircraft when he encountered Pilot Officer Harrington who greeted him with a heartfelt, 'I could do with a pint!'

Farmer Fred Lemon and his family at Alkmonton House Farm, had been alarmed by shouting and whistle blasts. Pilot Officer Gladwell, the pilot of WS683, Mr Lemon discovered, had parachuted into a field at nearby Park Style Farm then found Pilot Officer Bayley firmly snagged in an oak at Alkmonton Bottoms. With the help of the fire service, Pilot Officer Bayley was eventually released, when Mr Lemon took both crew members to his wife, Joan, for much-welcomed cups of tea.

'Pieces of aircraft,' remembered Mrs Barbara Grave, who lived in Sudbury Prison married-quarters, 'littered the ground in both the Prison and the Park.'

VISITING THE SITE

Tracing this train of events provides a good spread of flat walks, but with nothing to be seen of the incident at any of the sites. By 2013 even the spliced power cables, which remained for many years, had been renewed.

Meteor WS683 Sudbury Park (courtesy Derby Evening Telegraph)

Meteor WS621 in West Broughton Hollow (courtesy Derby Evening Telegraph)

Chinook HC3, ZA718
Rowsley, School Lane, Recreation Ground

SK25589 65536 351 feet.

Unit and Station: No. 18 Squadron, RAF Odiham

Date: 8 February, 2013

Crew:

- Flight Lieutenant Steve Hewer, pilot, captain
- Squadron Leader Matt D. Roberts, DFC, pilot (flying as weapon-systems officer [Wizzo])
- Sergeant Claire Burrows, air loadmaster/gunner
- Sergeant Alex Styling, air loadmaster/gunner

The Chinook in the playing field

The Chinook was about to enter the Wye Valley on a low-level exercise when a windscreen was damaged by a bird strike. The captain decided to put the machine down to have the damage repaired, landing on the recreation field off School Lane, Roseley, where it remained overnight until the damage was repaired.

The precautionary landing was made at 1500 hours, so children from the local school, as well as staff from the nearby Caudwell Mill Café, found their way over to visit, all subsequently expressing surprise at how welcome they had been made. The crew had, it seemed, done several tours in Afghanistan, but as this had been a training sortie setting down had been the politic way of handling the problem.

A while later the owner of the Mill received a print of the Chinook signed by all four crew members, and inscribed, 'Thank you to everybody for their kindness and generosity following our unplanned stop at Rowsley.'

This was, of course, in no sense a crash, but what it does bring out is the enlightened attitude to flight safety that so many wartime crews lacked. Had this been an operational sortie, without doubt the captain would have pressed on. And fifty and sixty years back there were a few captains who refused to descend blind through cloud ... But so few ...

AIR CRASH INVESTIGATION REPORTS

Specimen RAF air accident report summary, Form 1180, for Oxford V3210, Chapel-en-le-Frith area

Every aircraft accident, whether RAF or civil, generated a plethora of paperwork. Once a finding was reached, however, a summary of the investigation was produced. In 2013 the repository for the RAF summary reports (Form 1180) still extant was the RAF Museum, Hendon; while Squadron Operational Record Books and many full accident reports, civil and Service, were held by the Public Records Office, Kew. That many are missing is not due to some dastardly cover-up, but to the benign periodical pruning of archival material deemed, at the time, of no further interest. Conspiracy theorists should note too that air-crash investigations were carried out by relatively junior RAF officers who had little latitude in their reports. Above all, of course, it was in everyone's interest to disseminate throughout the RAF, the cause of any air accident.

Enthusiast researchers particularly complain about the inaccuracy of the recorded locations. But the precise location was never the investigators' primary concern. That was to establish the cause, so that a working reference sufficed to peg their report. This might be a bearing and distance; a statement, as illustrated, 'Wath on Dearne, 10 M Doncaster'; or a locale taken by word of mouth – as when Moorwood was recorded as Maud. (The example provided here, the sole occurrence in this series, when no location could be established, is intended as a memory-jogger). But the latter aside, once the debris was salvaged, burnt, or buried, who would ever be interested in where it had been? More particularly when the farmer was hovering, anxious to get his fields back into production.

However, a specific aim of this series is to furnish walkers with a dependable location. A location determined by a combination of (re-exposed) debris pools, metal detecting, documentary evidence, witness interviews, and memorials. A location, moreover, backed by GPS, a boon unavailable to such stalwarts as pioneering researcher Ron Collier, and beyond the dreams of the original salvage crews, not infrequently 'uncertain of their position' themselves.

'DARKY' EMERGENCY HOMING, AND ASSOCIATED EQUIPMENTS

Transmitter Receiver TR9,

Transmitter Receiver 1196

Throughout this series various emergency 'get-you-home' systems are mentioned, and 'Darky' in particular. This was a quintessentially British facility which made a strength out of the limited, twenty-five mile range of the airborne R/T (voice) radio installations of the day, the Transmitter Receiver TR9s and TR1196s carried by fighters and multi-crew aircraft respectively. The facility was operated at RAF stations, but also at certain Royal Observation Corps posts, button 'D' being the emergency channel on which a lost aircraft could transmit blind for 'Darky'. Any listening post hearing the call would respond with its position, thus furnishing the aircrew with a location accurate to twenty-five miles, often enough to enable them to plot a course for base. Alternatively, especially if the aircraft needed to land quickly, the ground station could pass it the course to the nearest airfield. The ground station would then phone the adjoining listening post in that direction, who, when it heard the aircraft call, would take over and refine the lead-in.

Among non-radio aids were 'Occults', aerial lighthouses radiating a white, periodically-shaded (or occluded) light flashing a single identifying letter, and visible at 30 miles, which could direct their beams towards the nearest airfield.

'Granite' was supplementary to both facilities, the station sending off red flares to show its position, or alternatively to warn of high ground.

By the end of hostilities the Royal Observer Corps proudly claimed that over 7,000 Allied aircraft were saved by use of such systems, with 1,800 other damaged machines being guided to safe landings.

THE 'QUEEN MARY' TRAILER, THE FORDSON TRACTOR; HORSEPOWER, 1944

The 'Queen Mary' trailer.

In 1938 Air Ministry tendered for a recovery vehicle which could carry a complete fighter aircraft. Within ten days Taskers Trailers of Andover submitted both a design and a prototype vehicle. Their bid was successful, and over 4,000 of their low-loading – 12 inch ground clearance – trailers were built. Regarding handling them, *The Reluctant Erk* (see Selective References) has a new airman-driver declaring, 'Anybody that tells you he's backed an articulator round a corner's a liar. He just happened to get one that was going round there anyhow.'

The Fordson tractor

The Fordson tractor which some farmers were able to use in helping to retrieve crashed aircraft is always referred to as a prized possession, and often the only one in the area, bringing it home that at the time the term horsepower on most British farms meant just that.

Horsepower, 1944. Horsepower, 1944. Jess, with Mr Alan Waller of Blaze Farm, Wildboarclough, courtesy of Harold and Florence Waller

CRASH-SITE PERSPEX SCULPTURE

Ring from Conksbury

It may be that the urge to collect souvenirs from crashed aircraft entered the human psyche when a fisherman retrieved some waxed feathers after Icarus disobeyed PROs (Paternal Flying Orders), broke away from Daedalus, and flew too near the sun. Certainly it flourished during the Second World War, when many a latter-day Icarus fell within the Peaklands, and indeed after it, judging from post-war pleas made for the return of souvenirs by crash investigators.

Most debris taken from the moors, then as now, finished up in dustbins, but in researching this series it became evident that perspex from turrets and cockpit canopies was fashioned into artefacts, into cigarette boxes, pendants, and most frequently, rings. Former exponents of the art described how fragments would be pierced with pokers heated in domestic coal fires, then filed into shape, and sometimes polished. An isolated variation was the use of aluminium tubing, but perspex was the material of choice.

Perhaps it is germane to point out that Daedalus, experiencing the same atmospheric conditions as his son, kept safety in mind, and made a successful flight.

The Conksbury ring was one of those fashioned from Wellington L7811 by Halifax flight engineer John James (Jim) Lomas and presented to his mother and to his sister, Joan Lomas, later Mrs Joan Dale, of Conksbury. An equally fine example was from a crashed German aircraft at Newhaven, retrieved and crafted by then-schoolgirl Beryl Mellor, of Friden. As Beryl, long since Mrs Beryl Rush, of Youlgreave, remembered, 'It was all the rage to make rings. I didn't use a poker, but I'd sit with newspaper on my knees, filing away for hours.' On the other hand the ring and the Mosquito from Chapel-en-le-Frith were fashioned by Pupil Pilot William Vincent Barrett, who survived the war as a flight sergeant on No. 17 Squadron. Most examples, however, were made by then-schoolboy creators who subsequently sold – or bartered – their products to local lasses.

Halifax Flight Engineer Jim Lomas, Youlgreave

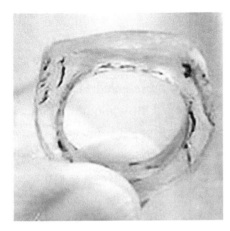

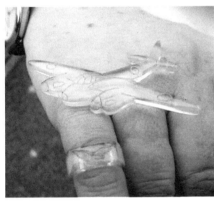

Top left: Ring from Youlgreave

Top right: *Mrs Beryl Rush (née Mellor), Youlgreave*

Bottom left: *Objects Chapel-en-le-Frith*

Bottom right: *William Barrett, Chapel-en-le-Frith*

AIRCRAFT TYPES

This section aims to provide the moorland walker-reader with a (very) potted guide to the once-proud aircraft now represented, at best, by mere shards of debris. Arabic numbers are employed throughout in designating aircraft marks, the problem of deciphering Roman numerals being left to the enthusiast. As for performance figures, published sources dealing with wartime aircraft often perpetuate values enhanced for propaganda purposes. But then even those quoted in *Pilot's Notes* incorporate a healthy safety margin, while workaday machines of a given type differ significantly.

Airspeed Oxford

The 1937 twin-engined, wooden-framed, plywood-skinned Airspeed Oxford remained in RAF Service until 1954. A dual-controlled, general purpose trainer, it had a basic crew of three but could accommodate other trainee-aircrew depending upon the role.

Two 375 horsepower Armstrong Siddeley Cheetah Ten radial engines, or alternatively, two 450 horsepower Pratt & Witney radial engines, gave it a cruising speed of some 163 mph (142 knots) and a ceiling of 19,000 feet; range was 700 miles. It could carry practice bombs and a few had a dorsal turret with a single 0.303 inch (7.7 mm) calibre machine gun.

Auster Autocrat

The Auster Autocrat was a three-seater cabin-monoplane with a high-set braced wing and a fixed, tailwheel-configured undercarriage. Essentially, it was the same as the wartime Taylorcraft Air Observation Post version. Powered by a Cirrus Minor Mk.2 90 bhp air-cooled engine, it took off at 40 mph (35 knots), climbed at 65 mph (56 knots), cruised at 85 mph (74 knots), and was normally descended at 40 mph (35 knots) in a powered approach. Not particularly inspiring to fly, it was, nevertheless both dependable and docile.

Avro Anson

The 1935 Anson stayed with the RAF for 22 years. Conceived as a maritime reconnaissance aircraft, it was withdrawn from operational service in early 1942, after which it was employed extensively in the training role. As a dual-controlled machine with such innovations as hydraulically-operated flaps and undercarriage, it was used to train most aircrew specialisations. Normally accommodating between three and five, it could also be configured as an eight- to eleven-seat communications aircraft.

The Anson was well liked, being easy to fly, dependable, sturdy, and relatively forgiving. Its performance on one engine, however, was poor.

The Anson was typically powered by two 350 horsepower Armstrong Siddeley Cheetah Nine radial engines which gave it a cruising speed of 158 mph (138 knots) and a ceiling of 19,000 feet. Its range was nearly 800 miles.

Avro Shackleton MR.3

The 1949 Avro Shackleton, retaining the proven strengths of the Lancaster, joined the squadrons in April 1951. When the Nimrod patrol aircraft assumed the maritime task in 1971 the Shackleton was employed as an Airborne Early Warning platform until, in 1991, the Boeing E3D Sentry took over. The Shackleton was constantly updated, not least when the tricycle undercarriage was introduced on the Mark 3 in 1955.

The Shackleton was typically powered by four Rolls-Royce Griffon Mk.57A in-line piston engines, each of which developed 2,455 horsepower. In round terms it had a maximum take-off weight of 98,000 pounds, a ceiling of 19,000 feet, a fuel capacity of 4,258 gallons, an endurance of nearly fifteen hours, and a range of some 3,500 miles. Its maximum speed was 300 mph (261 knots) and it cruised at 180-240 mph (156-209 knots) depending upon the task in hand.

Typical of its armament was two 20 mm calibre cannon in the nose, and two machine guns at the tail. It carried up to 10,000 pounds of bombs or depth charges, and was normally operated by a crew of ten.

Avro Tutor

The Avro Tutor was the RAF's standard elementary trainer from 1932 until 1939. Fabric covered over welded steel-tube construction, it was typically powered by a 240 horsepower Armstrong Siddeley Lynx Mk.4C radial engine screened by an aerodynamically-enhancing Townend ring. It had a maximum speed of 122 mph (106 knots), cruised at 105 mph (91 knots), could reach 15,000 feet in 32 minutes, had a range of 250 miles, and a ceiling of 16,200 feet.

It was ahead of its age, having features which later trainers lacked: a self-centring tailwheel, adjustable seats and rudder pedals, a variable-incidence all-flying tailplane, and efficient brakes. Further to this, care had been taken to make it easily accessible for servicing.

In all, it seems, it was a gentleman's aircraft, and well liked, but if anything just a little too docile and forgiving for a trainer.

BE2C

Geoffrey de Havilland designed the Royal Aircraft Factory's 1914 two-seater BE2C as a reconnaissance and bombing machine. A development of the Factory's earlier BE (Blériot Experimental) models, it introduced ailerons instead of wing-warping for lateral control. Specifically designed as a stable, easy-to-fly machine it, therefore, lacked manoeuvrability. Despite this it was chosen for mass production, a decision which was to cost the Royal Flying Corps many casualties. Notwithstanding which the BE2C was retained on the Western Front until 1917, and only then retired to home defence and training duties.

Typical of several power sources was the 90 horsepower Royal Aircraft Factory in-line, air-cooled engine which gave the BE2C a ceiling of 10,000 feet with a working maximum speed of 72 mph (63 knots). It carried a single machine gun – unlike its predecessors from the RAF (the Factory's altogether too-confusing abbreviation) which had been unarmed – and could carry 224 pounds of bombs mounted on underwing racks.

Boeing B-17 Flying Fortress

The Boeing B-17 first flew in July 1935, when its perceived role was that of a long-range outpost capable of defending America beyond the range of its shore defences, hence 'Flying Fortress'. However, after it was tested in action with the RAF such modifications as self-sealing fuel tanks and an increased amount of protective armour were called for. With these installed the B-17 then became the mainstay of the United States Eighth Army Air Force's bombing campaign which began in August 1942.

The enormous tail fin ensured that it was stable at great heights, while the fact that it had formidable defensive armament, and that it proved capable of absorbing a considerable amount of battle damage, was held to make up for its relatively small bomb load.

The upgraded B-17G version relied for its defence on up to thirteen 0.5 inch, heavy-calibre machine guns, this fire-power being enhanced by the interdependent formation strategies employed. With so many guns to man, the standard crew complement was ten. This comprised pilot, co-pilot, navigator, bombardier, flight engineer, and radio operator. In combat the flight engineer would man the top turret, and the radio operator a swivel-gun in the roof of his compartment. The remaining four crew were dedicated gunners to man the ball-turret, the left and right waist positions, and the tail turret.

Typical performance figures for the B-17 reflect that it was powered by four 1,200 horsepower Wright Cyclone R-1820-65 9-cylinder air-cooled engines, with Hamilton three-bladed, constant-speed, fully-feathering propellers. This combination gave it a cruising speed of 225 mph (196 knots), a ceiling of over 40,000 feet, and a normal range of 3,000 miles. Its standard bomb load was 6,000 pounds, although this could be increased to 12,800 pounds, and over a very short range, to 20,800 pounds – for a comparison often made, the Lancaster's standard bomb load was 14,000 pounds, and it could be adapted to carry one bomb weighing 22,000 pounds.

Boulton Paul Defiant

The 1937 Boulton Paul Defiant, a low-wing, all-metal, twin-crewed fighter, had four 0.303 inch (7.7 mm) calibre machine guns mounted in a moveable dorsal turret. This meant, though, that it had neither belly nor head-on protection, additionally, its performance was penalised by the weight and drag of the turret. In December 1940 it was withdrawn from daylight operations but once re-employed as a night-fighter, and particularly when equipped with airborne-interception radar, it was to be more successful. Later it served as a target tug.

With a 1,280 horsepower Rolls-Royce Merlin Mk.20 engine it could cruise at 260 mph (226 knots) and climb to some 30,000 feet. It had a range of 465 miles and a maximum take-off weight of 8,424 pounds.

Bristol Blenheim

In 1935 air-minded Lord Rothermere's private runabout proved to be faster than the RAF's latest fighters. By 1937 it had become the three-crewed, twin-engined Blenheim light bomber which would equip seventy RAF squadrons. By 1939, however, it was far outclassed by German fighters. Although quickly withdrawn from bombing operations it continued to serve as a radar-equipped night-fighter, and later, as an advanced crew trainer.

Employing two 905 horsepower Bristol Mercury Fifteen radial engines, the Blenheim Mk.4 had a ceiling of 27,000 feet, a cruising speed of 198 mph (172 knots), and a range of 1,460 miles. Armed with two 0.303 inch (7.7 mm) calibre machine guns in a power-operated dorsal turret, with two remotely-controlled guns below the nose, and a fifth in the port wing, it could also carry a 1,300 pound load of bombs.

Bristol Fighter Mk.3

The 1916 Bristol Fighter Mk.2B – from the outset 'Fighter', and never 'Scout' – had a disastrous baptism of fire, after which the Royal Flying Corps learnt to use it for offence rather than defence. The post-war RAF adopted it as the standard army co-operation machine, and in 1926 restructured Mk 2s were re-designated Mk.3s.

The two-seater biplane fighter, wooden framed, and with fabric covering, was powered by a 275 horsepower Rolls-Royce Falcon 3 engine which gave it a maximum speed of 123 mph (107 knots), a time to 10,000 feet of twelve minutes, a ceiling of 20,000 feet, and an endurance of three hours. It had a touch-down speed of 45 mph (39 knots).

It carried a synchronised Vickers 0.303 inch calibre machine gun firing through the propeller, and at least one Lewis machine gun mounted on a Scarff Ring in the rear cockpit, additionally it could carry 240 pounds of bombs. It remained in service until 1932.

Canadair Argonaut

The 1938 Argonaut was derived from the Douglas DC4 which became the military C-54 Skymaster. Its sponsor airline found the Argonaut 'complicated to maintain and uneconomical to operate', the future spin rendering this, 'ahead of its time'. And it had much to offer, not least a constant cross-section fuselage, with easy access as an incidental benefit of a nosewheel undercarriage. Post war, several pressurised DC4s with Rolls-Royce engines were built for the British Overseas Airways Corporation by Canadair.

Powered by four Rolls-Royce Merlin engines it had a cruising speed of 227 mph (197 knots), a ceiling of 22,300 feet, and was able to lift a payload of 11,440 pounds over a range of some 6,500 miles. Its normal complement was three flight-deck crew, four cabin staff, and 44 passengers.

Cessna 150

The strut-braced, high-winged, tricycle-undercarriaged, two-seater Cessna 150 first flew in September 1957, after which over 30,000 were built with up to 20,000 still flying in 2013. Pleasant to handle, forgiving, viceless, and dependable, it built up a reputation for being the most popular light aeroplane ever produced.

A 100 horsepower Continental 0-200A flat-four engine driving a two-bladed fixed-pitch propeller gave it an average cruising speed of 122 mph (106 knots) with 65-70 mph (56-61 knots) sufficing for virtually all manoeuvring. The ceiling was 15,000 feet and the range 350 miles.

Chinook Helicopter; Boeing H3C

A 1960s design of tandem-rotor, heavy-lift support helicopter whose technical, armament, and electronic fit allows it to undertake an extremely wide range of tasks. It can carry up to 55 troops or ten tonnes of freight, alternatively, two Land Rovers, or 24 stretchers.

An typical operational crew is a pilot, a co-pilot or weapon systems officer (Wizzo), with two air loadmaster/gunners.

Two Textron Lycoming T55-L712F turboshaft engines each provide a thrust of 3,148 shaft horsepower giving a 15,000 feet ceiling and a speed of some 170 knots (196 mph).

De Havilland DH10

The de Havilland DH10, the Amiens, had a troubled existence. Production delays meant it hardly saw service in World War One, and it was never a success. It did, however, serve in various policing roles, but among de Havilland ventures it was very much a nonentity.

A three-seater, twin-engined biplane long-range day-bomber, it was fitted with two 400 horsepower Liberty 12 engines, which, according to the contemporary *Jane's*, gave it a speed 'low down' of 128 mph (111 knots), one of 117 mph (102 knots) at 15,000 feet, and allowed it to carry ordnance weighing 1,248 pounds. Other sources add that its ceiling was 17,500 feet, and its duration six hours. For defensive armament it carried two Lewis 0.303 inch calibre machine guns, one in the nose, and another amidships.

De Havilland DH60X Cirrus Moth

The first of the two-seater, single-engined de Havilland Moth biplane family made its initial flight in February 1925, powered by a Cirrus engine. This power plant was never truly satisfactory but the X Version (X for experimental) sought to improve it. The popularity of the Moth – owners could fold back the wings for storage – encouraged the development of the Gipsy engine, after which the type became generically known as the Gipsy Moth.

Representative of the type's performance was a maximum speed of 105 mph (91 knots) at sea level, a cruise of 85 mph (74 knot), a ceiling of 18,000 feet and a range of some 300 miles.

De Havilland DH82A Tiger Moth

The 1934 improved Service version of the tandem two-seater biplane de Havilland Moth made an unassailable name for itself as a training machine at over eighty elementary flying training schools in the course of the Second World War.

Its 130 horsepower de Havilland Gipsy Major in-line engine gave it a cruising speed of 93 mph (80 knots), a ceiling of 13,000 feet and a range of 300 miles. Equipped with a hood to facilitate instrument flying, it could be fitted with bomb racks, and indeed, saw operational service both as a communications aircraft before the fall of France, and as a maritime scout.

For solo flight the pilot sat in the rear seat to maintain the centre of gravity. Although demanding to fly accurately, it had virtually no vices, just the same, it brooked no undue liberties. Examples of the type still flew in 2013, and it is almost universally spoken of reverentially. It might be held as sacrilegious, therefore, to recall that its cockpit was uncomfortable, and that it invariably gave a freezing-cold ride.

De Havilland DH85 Leopard Moth

The 1933 Leopard Moth was a three-seater, high-winged monoplane with an enclosed cabin accommodating two side-by-side passenger seats behind the pilot. It was powered by a 130-horsepower de Havilland Gipsy-Major four-cylinder, in-line, air-cooled inverted engine which gave it a maximum speed of 138 mph (120 knots), an initial climb rate of 625 feet a minute, a ceiling of 17,300 feet, and a range of 715 miles. Sales were helped when a Leopard Moth won the 1933 King's Cup air race two weeks after its first flight.

De Havilland Vampire

The 1946 twin-boomed de Havilland Vampire, the third of Britain's jet aircraft, was a private de Havilland venture which had a lot in common with the Mosquito, the whole forward zone being predominantly aluminium-skinned wood. Nippy, yet essentially stable and easy to fly, the Vampire, and particularly the Mk.5 fighter-bomber variant (as at Torgate Farm), also proved a useful stop-gap advanced trainer for Flying Training Command. The dedicated twin-seat, side-by-side trainer version, the T.11 ('Tee Eleven'), became available in 1950.

The T.11, with its Goblin 3 centrifugal-flow, turbo-jet engine developing 3,200 pounds of static thrust, had a maximum permitted speed of 523 mph (455 knots), a medium-level cruising speed of 265 mph (230 knots), a range of 730 miles, and it was to remain in RAF service until 1966. Although nominally a trainer it could mount two or four 20 mm calibre cannon, and provision was made to carry rocket projectiles or bombs.

Douglas Boston, or Havoc

The American A-20 was variously employed as medium bomber, fighter-bomber, night-fighter and night intruder. The crew comprised pilot, navigator, and gunner.

Twin 1,600 horsepower Wright Cyclone engine gave a top speed of 304 mph (264 knots), a cruise of 250 mph (217 knots), a ceiling of 24,250 feet. The range was 1,020 miles and its maximum bomb load two 1,000 pound bombs.

Representative armament was four fixed 0.303 inch (7.7 mm) calibre machine guns in the nose with another two pairs in the dorsal and ventral positions. The Boston was the first RAF operational aircraft to have a tricycle undercarriage.

Fairey Battle

Although relatively impressive when it first flew in early 1936, the single-engined Fairey Battle light-bomber was already obsolete by 1939 when war broke out. Accommodating a pilot, bomb-aimer/observer, and a wireless operator/air gunner, the Battle, powered by a 1,030 horsepower Rolls-Royce Merlin Mk.1 in-line engine, cruised at 210 mph (182 knots) at up to 25,000 feet and had a range of 1,000 miles. It had a bomb load of 1,000 pounds.

For defence it had a Vickers 0.303 inch calibre machine gun in a rear-cockpit mounting, and another in the starboard wing. It was totally outclassed by the German first-line fighters, however, and after a series of gallantly fought, but disastrous, engagements during the German advance into France, the Battle was withdrawn as a day bomber. It continued to serve, however, in the training and target-towing roles.

Handley Page Hampden

The 1936 four-crewed Hampden, powered by two 1,000 horsepower, 9-cylinder, Bristol Pegasus Mark Eighteen radial engines, equipped ten RAF bomber squadrons at the outbreak of war. Here, though, is a case where propaganda-enhanced performance figures refuse to lie dormant. So, the Hampden's ceiling is frequently given as 19,000 feet, although Handley Page themselves only claimed 15,000 feet. At the same time, they extolled their product's 'incredibly fast' 254 mph (221 knots) maximum speed. But although a 1942 source gives the cruise as 217 mph (189 knots), actual users found the workaday cruise to be nearer 130 mph (113 knots), with the least sanguine modern source proffering 167 mph (145 knots).

Irreconcilable figures aside, the Hampden's Handley Page leading-edge slots did give it a landing speed of just 73 mph (64 knots), and most sources agree that at a maximum take-off weight of 18,756 pounds it had a range of 1,885 miles with half a bomb load, reducing to 1,200 miles when the full 4,000 pounds was carried. As defensive armament it mounted two forward-firing 0.303 inch (7.7 mm) calibre machine guns, with additional twin mountings in both a dorsal and a rearward-facing belly position.

The Hampden performed poorly against German fighters, however, and just a month into the war it was restricted to night operations, to leaflet dropping, and to minelaying. Although the Hampden was regarded as pleasant to handle, the crew found their positions cramped.

Handley Page Heyford

The 1933 twin-engined, normally four-crewed Heyford, was a biplane-bomber of all-metal, framed construction whose speedy 143 mph (124 knots) earned it the appellation, 'Express'. Indeed, unlikely as it seems, a No.102 Squadron Heyford was publicly looped during the 1935 Hendon Air Show! Interestingly too, it was held – admittedly by Handley Page – that, in comparison to a retractable undercarriage, the lighter weight of the streamlined but fixed-undercarriage so minimised drag that it actually enhanced the Heyford's performance. Withdrawn from first-line service in 1939 the type still gave good value as a crew trainer until 1941, being stable, and pleasant to fly.

Powered by two 575 horsepower, Rolls-Royce Kestrel Mk.3 engines the Heyford had a ceiling of 21,000 feet and could carry up to 3,500 pounds of bombs. With half this bomb load it had an operational striking range of 920 miles, or, according to Handley Page, 'carried a very large load of bombs for 2,000 miles'. For defensive armament it had three 0.303 inch (7.7 mm) calibre Lewis machine guns mounted respectively in dorsal, ventral, and nose positions.

Hawker Audax

The 1931 Audax was the army co-operation variant of the Hart. The RAF received the Audax in February 1932, using it mainly as an advanced trainer. Some, however, were used during the Second World War, notably in Iraq in May 1941 when RAF Habbaniyah, then the largest station in the Service, was besieged by Iraqi rebels.

The Audax was typically powered by a 530 horsepower Rolls-Royce Kestrel engine, had a maximum speed of 170 mph (148 knots), could climb to 10,000 feet in some ten minutes, had a ceiling of 21,000 feet and an endurance of three and half hours. It could carry a bomb load of 230 pounds and was armed with a forward-firing Vickers machine gun and an aft-mounted Lewis, both of 0.303 inch calibre.

Heinkel He111

The 1935 Heinkel He111 ('one-eleven') was blooded with the Condor Legion in the Spanish Civil War, and later in Poland. Over Britain, however, both its armament and performance proved inadequate, particularly as

German fighters were unable to dwell long enough to provide meaningful support. From mid-September 1940, therefore, it was restricted to night-time operations.

Powered by two 1100 Junkers Jumo engines it had an average speed (collating various sources) of 250 mph (217 knots), a ceiling of 23,000 feet, and a range of 1,030 miles. Early versions had a crew of four, a bomb load of some 4,000 pounds and were armed with three 7.9 mm calibre machine guns mounted dorsally, in the nose, and in a belly turret.

Junkers Ju88

Fortunately for the Allies, German aircraft designers, like their British counterparts, frequently had changes forced upon them. The 1939 Junkers Ju88 bomber, for example, was envisaged as a fast, minimally-armed machine capable of targeting the whole of the British Isles. In the event, the Luftwaffe's insistence that it be used primarily as a dive bomber called for a more robust construction. This increased the weight and reduced the design speed and manoeuvrability, reductions which called for more defensive armament. The bitter pill being that the type was never actually used as a dive-bomber except when operating over water!

Two 1,400 horsepower Junkers 211J liquid-cooled inverted V12 engines gave a maximum speed of 295 mph (256 knots) and a ceiling of 26,900 feet. The four crew comprised pilot, bomb aimer, top-gunner/radio-operator, and lower-gunner/flight-engineer. Armament was a 7.9 mm calibre gun under the control of the pilot, together with three 7.9 mm calibre guns and a 13 mm calibre gun fought by the gunners. Four 1,000 kilogram bombs could be carried.

Klemm Kl.35

The 1935 Klemm Kl.35 gull-winged monoplane, with steel-framed fuselage and wooden wings, was reputed to have excellent handling qualities and good visibility. Designer Klemm had set out to make a popular aeroplane that was as economical to run as a car, as easy to manufacture and maintain, and small enough to fit in a garage. As a consequence most German pilots during the 20s and 30s trained on Klemms. Interestingly, although an early and enthusiastic Nazi Party member, Klemm later fell foul of the Gestapo. Just the same, he survived the war.

The Kl.36 was powered by a 105 horsepower Hirth HM504-A2 four-cylinder air-cooled engine which gave it a maximum speed of 130 mph (113 knots) and a ceiling of 14,400 feet. It had a cruising speed of 118 mph (103 knots), and a landing speed of 48 mph (42 knots).

Miles Magister

The 1936 tandem-seated, low-winged, metal-skinned Miles Hawk mono-plane so impressed the RAF that a Service version, the Magister elementary trainer, was ordered. A serious spinning problem was encountered, and solved, and other modifications were made.

Powered by a 130 horsepower de Havilland Gipsy Major One in-line engine, it had a cruising speed of 123 mph (107 knots), ceiling of 18,000 feet, and a range of 380 miles. It boasted wheelbrakes, power-operated flaps, and a tailwheel – as opposed to a skid –, and could be flown solo from either seat, although the front seat was preferred.

Unlike its contemporary, the Tiger Moth, it responded well in gusty conditions. On the other hand, unless controlled, the Hawk's wing would lift markedly in a crosswind. Then again there were trimming controls to master. Just two of the 'complications' that made it a good trainer. And there were no vices. Only, for all its good points, it never aroused anything like the affection engendered by the Tiger Moth.

Miles Master Mk. 3

When the 1935 private-venture Miles Kestrel showed a top speed of nearly 300 mph – just twenty miles an hour slower than the Hurricane – it seemed the ideal machine for easing the transition from the Tiger Moth and Magister trainers to the first-line Hurricanes and Spitfires. However, following a pattern only too well established even by then, so many modifications were called for that in March 1939, when the emergent Miles Master trainer first flew, it was a full hundred miles an hour slower than the Hurricane. It did, however, retain handling characteristics similar to those of the new fighters.

After engine-fit problems, the Master Mark Three received the 825 horsepower Pratt & Whitney Wasp Junior radial, which gave the tandem-seated trainer a maximum speed of 232 mph (202 knots) and a cruising speed of 170 mph (148 knots) while retaining the 85 mph (74 knots) landing speed of earlier marks. It also had a ceiling of 25,000 feet and a range of 390 miles.

Gloster Meteor

Celebrated for being the only Allied jet aircraft to see service during the Second World War, the twin-jet Meteor fighter first flew in March 1943. Due to developmental delays, however, deliveries only began in July 1944, after which it was successfully deployed against the V1 Flying Bombs.

A two-seater trainer was produced in 1948, while periodic updating of equipment included the provision of Martin Baker ejection seats.

Early versions were powered by two Rolls-Royce Welland turbojet engines, each developing 1,700 pounds of static thrust, which gave a top speed of 415 mph (361 knots) and a ceiling of 40,000 feet. Later versions, fitted with the more powerful Rolls-Royce Derwent 8 engines, each giving 3,660 pounds of thrust, brought the speed up to nearly 600 mph (521 Knots) and gave an initial rate of climb of 7,350 feet a minute.

Noorduyn Norseman

The Canadian-manufactured, single-engined, ten-seater Noorduyn Norseman UC-64A was widely used by the United States Army Air Force as a light transport. Having first flown in 1935 it was a veteran design even in 1944, but it was rugged, adaptable, and always dependable. Just the same, it was to gain undeserved notoriety as the type in which bandleader Major Glenn Miller disappeared over the English Channel on 15 December 1944.

The Norseman was powered by a 600 horsepower Pratt & Whitney engine which gave it a cruising speed of 148 mph (129 knots) and a maximum speed of 162 mph (141 knots). It had a ceiling of 17,000 feet and a range of 1,150 miles.

North American Harvard

17,000 of the 1935-vintage Harvards were built, far more than of any other wartime trainer. Both Britain and France ordered them, the Luftwaffe using the former French machines for training but also for familiarising pilots tasked with evaluating captured American machines. Though the Harvard remained in RAF service from January 1939 until 1955, the South African Air Force retained it until 1995!

A 550/600 horsepower, 9-cylinder & Whitney Wasp air-cooled engine driving a Hamilton two-bladed, two-position controllable-pitch propeller gave a cruising speed of 180 mph (156 knots). The landing speed was 63 mph (55 knots) with an initial climb rate of 1,350 feet a minute. The ceiling was 23,000 feet, the range 730 miles, and the maximum weight 2,260 pounds.

Handley Page Harrow

The Harrow, a four- to five-seater, twin-finned, monoplane bomber, first flew in October 1936, but being obsolescent when war broke out in 1939, initially served as a bomber-trainer before being re-deployed as a transport.

Its twin 925 horsepower Bristol Pegasus Twenty radial engines powered it to a 163 mph (142 knots) cruising speed and gave it a 22,800 feet ceiling. It could carry a bomb load of 3,000 pounds and was armed with four 0.303 inch calibre machine guns, two in the tail turret, and one each in nose and dorsal positions. The Harrow had a range of 1,250 miles and was to make its most telling contribution by evacuating casualties during the ill-fated Arnhem operation in September 1944, its Handley-Page leading-edge slots permitting it to operate from fields which were far too small for other heavy aircraft.

Republic P-47 Thunderbolt

Republic's 1941 P-47 Thunderbolt high-altitude, medium- to long-range escort fighter began operating in Europe in early 1943 and quickly proved its worth. Indeed, from March 1944, with its range extended by droppable tanks, it was able to escort the bombers on round-trip raids upon Berlin.

The Thunderbolt was typically powered by a 2,000 horsepower turbo-supercharged Pratt & Whitney Double Wasp air-cooled engine driving a four-bladed Curtiss constant-speed, fully-feathering propeller. This combination gave it a maximum speed of some 433 mph (376 knots), an initial climb rate of 2,805 feet a minute, a ceiling of over 40,000 feet, and a range greater than 1,700 miles.

It was armed with eight wing-mounted 0.5 inch calibre machine guns and could also fire rocket projectiles or deliver two 1,000 pound bombs from underwing mountings.

McDonnell-Douglas Phantom RF-4C

The Phantom RF-4C, whose prototype first flew in August 1963, was the unarmed photographic-reconnaissance version of the Phantom F-4C fighter, the most noticeable external difference being its longer, sharper nose. Within the modified machine, however, the armament and radar of the fighter was replaced by specialised photographic-reconnaissance equipment. This included various dedicated cameras, side-looking ground-mapping radar, infra-red imaging equipment for the reconnaissance role, a photoflash ejection system for night photography, and radar with both terrain-avoidance and terrain-following modes. Additionally, there were infra-red and laser target-designators to provide slant range, and high-resolution thermal-imaging equipment.

The Phantom was powered by two General Electric J79-GE-15 turbojets, each of 10,300 pounds static thrust, or 17,000 pounds with afterburner. This combination gave it a maximum speed of 1,459 mph (1,268 knots) at 48,000 feet, that is, Mach 2.21 (2.21 times the local speed of sound); and 834 mph (725 knots) at sea level, or Mach 1.09. Cruising speed was 587 mph (510 knots), and landing speed 143 mph (124 knots).

The initial rate of climb varied enormously with the version, also with what 'stores' were carried, figures varying from 28,000 to 46,000 feet a minute, and even higher. A typical service ceiling is given as 59,400 feet, a combat range 840 miles, and a ferry range of 1,750 miles with full external fuel resources. Maximum take-off weight was some 58,000 pounds, and the maximum for engaging in combat, 39,773 pounds.

Percival Proctor Mk.3

The 1939 three-seater Proctor, a development of the four-seater 1935 Vega Gull, with flaps and dual controls, was used by both the RAF and the Royal

Navy for communications and radio training, some acting in the taxi role for the Metropolitan Communications Squadron at Hendon until 1955.

Powered by a 210 horsepower de Havilland Gipsy Queen in-line engine, it had a maximum speed of 160 mph (139 knots), a cruising speed of 140 mph (122 knots), a range of 500 miles, and a ceiling of 14,000 feet.

Pierre Robin R1180TD Aiglon

This was a relatively short-lived variant of the 1972 Robin DR400, built in 1978. A four-seater, it was powered by a Lycoming 0-360 engine which gave it a maximum speed of some 155 mph (135 knots), a cruising speed of 136 mph (118 knots), a ceiling of 12,000 feet, and an initial rate of climb of 600 feet a minute. Handling was, by design, more stable than lively, while the canopy afforded a striking all-round view.

Republic F-84 Thunderstreak

The swept-wing, all-flying-tail, F-84 ground-support fighter-bomber was developed from the straight-winged F-84, the prototype flying in June 1950. Engine, and handling and stability problems, however, delayed deliveries until 1954. In the 1960s it was replaced by the F-100, but lingered on with the United States National Guard until 1971.

A typical engine fit was the Wright J65-W-3, the licence-built adaptation of the British Armstrong Siddeley Sapphire, whose 7,220 pounds of thrust gave the weighty 27,000 pound Thunderstreak an initial climb rate of 7,400 feet a minute, a maximum speed of 685 mph (595 knots) and a ceiling of 44,450 feet. The limiting Mach number was M1.18 in a dive, the range some 1,900 miles, and the cruising speed 535 mph (465 knots).

Armament was six 0.5 inch calibre machine guns, one in each wing and four in the nose, and twenty-four five-inch rockets; with up to 6,000 pounds of externally carried ordnance.

Short Stirling

The 1941 Short Stirling was the first of the RAF's heavy bombers. Shorts re-used their successful Sunderland-wing profile but Ministry requirements limited the span to 100 feet (not, as myth has it, to fit into RAF hangars, these being 125 feet wide!). This, and similar modifications, detracted from the design performance to give the Stirling a ceiling of only 17,000 feet. It was, however, very manoeuvrable, and powered by four 1,650 horsepower Bristol Hercules Sixteen radial engines, had a maximum speed of 270 mph (235 knots), a cruise of 200 mph (174 knots) and a range – dependent upon bomb load – of up to 2,000 miles.

It carried 14,000 pounds of bombs, and had eight 0.303 inch (7.7 mm) calibre machine guns; four in a tail turret, and two each in nose and dorsal turrets. Its cockpit stood at a lofty 22 feet 9 inches above the tarmac.

Though popular with its seven- or eight-man crews, its bomb bay could not be adapted as bigger bombs were developed and it ceased bomber operations in September 1941. It was then very successfully employed in the glider-tug, clandestine-operations, and transport roles.

Supermarine Spitfire

The Spitfire first flew on 5 March 1936 and by October 1947, when production ceased, had metamorphosed through over a score of variant Marks. The late-1940 Mk.2 was powered by a 1,150 horsepower Rolls-Royce Merlin Mark Twelve in-line engine. This gave it a maximum level speed of 355 mph (308 knots) and a cruising speed of 265 mph (230 knots). It took 7 minutes to reach 20,000 feet, its ceiling was 37,200 feet, and its range, on 85 gallons, 500 miles. It carried either eight 0.303 inch (7.7 mm) calibre machine guns, or two 20 mm calibre cannon together with four 0.303 inch machine guns. None of this would give a complete picture, however, unless the superb handling qualities of the machine were mentioned.

V1 (*Vergeltungswaffe*) Flying Bomb

The German *Fern Ziel Geraet*, (effectively: Long-range Aiming Apparatus), their *Vergeltungswaffe 1*, (Reprisal Weapon Number One), was a pilotless flying bomb. The V1 was propelled up a railed launching ramp by volatile hydrogen peroxide, and then accelerated to 410 mph (356 knots) by an Argus AS14 pulse-jet which developed 660 pounds of static thrust. 750 gallons of petrol gave the device a range of 150 miles, the total weight of 4,750 pounds including just under a ton of amatol high-explosive.

The pulse-jet engine operated using a system of shutter-type valves whose action gave the singular sound that, as any bombarded populace quickly learnt, heralded its approach. On reaching its target area the device was rigged to dive. As the nose dipped so the fuel flow was interrupted and the engine stopped, indicating to the initiated that only moments later the bomb would explode.

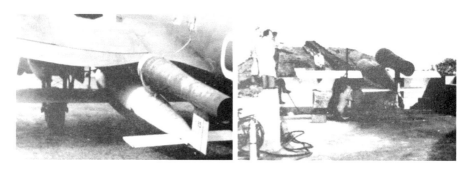

Left: V1 below He111; Right: V1 on launching pad

The main assault on Britain and Belgium began in June 1944 and lasted eighty days, some being fired as late as early 1945. It is generally held that of the 10,000 V1s launched against England, 7,000 landed on the mainland.

The defences comprised barrage balloons, aircraft, and anti-aircraft guns, but once especially adapted rangefinders became available, most V1s were shot down by the guns as they crossed the coast.

While normally ramp-launched against London and Antwerp from sites on the French coast, 825 V1s were carried beneath Heinkel He.111 bombers, some to be air-launched into the Peakland area.

For newer generations it might be politic to reiterate that while the V2 was a rocket, the V1 [these days, too-often termed 'V1 rocket'] was a pilotless, pulse-jet aircraft.

Vickers Armstrongs Wellington

In designing the 1937 Wellington, the celebrated Barnes Wallis used repeated junctions of Meccano-like alloy members to form a cocoon of great strength. This 'geodetic' – parts of a circle – structure was then covered with doped fabric. The operational crew of four comprised pilot, navigator/bomb-aimer, wireless operator/air gunner, and rear gunner.

The German defences soon took the Wellington's measure, after which it was switched to night bombing. However, Wellingtons were also employed in the maritime role.

A typical power fit was two 1,500 horsepower Bristol Hercules Eleven radial engines which gave a ceiling of 19,000 feet and a maximum speed of 235 mph (204 knots). Representative cruising speeds vary with source, ranging from 232 mph (202 knots) to 166 mph (144 knots). A former Wellington pilot suggested 173 mph (150 knots), with a normal bombing altitude of 12,000 feet.

The bomb load was 4,500 pounds and the armament eight 0.303 inch (7.7 mm) calibre machine guns; four in the tail turret, two in the beam, and two in the nose.

The Wellington continued in service until 1953 using the T.10 version which, with the nose turret faired over, was dedicated to the pilot and navigator training roles.

Westland Lysander

The 1936 Lysander was a purpose-designed, two-seater, army co-operation machine delivered to the RAF in 1938. By the outbreak of war seven squadrons were Lysander equipped but although some saw action prior to the fall of France, the use of First World War techniques and the fact that the enemy had air superiority, meant that losses were inordinately high.

As a consequence the type was withdrawn from first-line service but continued to serve as a target tug, and in the air-defence-co-operation and air-sea rescue roles. The Lysander, however, excelled as a clandestine delivery machine for the Special Operations Executive (SOE), where its short-field performance was well suited to landing supplies and personnel in occupied Europe.

With its cockpit standing fourteen-and-a-half feet above the ground the Lysander was typically powered by an 870 horsepower Bristol Mercury Twenty or Thirty radial engine which gave it a maximum speed of 212 mph (184 knots) and a ceiling of 21,500 feet. It had a range of 600 miles.

GLOSSARY

1. Aviation

Aberfan: village in Wales. On 21 October 1966 a slurry from a rain-soaked spoil heap killed 116 children and 28 adults. Other slag heaps were reduced for safety.

Air Defence of Great Britain Command: an inter-war formation which was resurrected from 15 November 1943 until 15 October 1944 when it became Fighter Command once more.

Bar (to a gallantry award): this term indicates a further award of a gallantry decoration and is represented by a rosette sewn to the ribbon. Not to be confused with the 'medal bar' or 'medal clasp' (denoting campaigns) running across the ribbon of a general service medal.

Bearings and fixes (radio): in essence, a bearing taken across track would show how far along track an aircraft had reached, while the intersection of bearings from two stations 'fixed' the aircraft's position. When radio silence was imposed bearings could be obtained by directional loop. Otherwise ground direction-finding stations could be asked for bearings.

Circuits and Rollers: a 'circuit' – circuits and landings – involves taking off into wind, turning downwind parallel to the runway, flying past the airfield, then turning back, touching down, and rolling to a stop before clearing the runway. A 'roller' (circuits and bumps), on the other hand, requires the pilot to touch down but, without coming to a halt, to put on full power, reconfigure the aircraft for flight, and take off again.

Cluster: a bronze oak cluster is a device worn on American medal ribbons to denote subsequent awards of a decoration and depicts a twig of four oak leaves with three acorns. A silver cluster denotes the award of five bronze clusters. The British equivalent is a bar – a rosette –, not to be confused with the bronze oak leaf of the Mention in Despatches (silver since 1993).

Darky: an emergency homing system making a benefit of the very short range of wartime voice-radio sets. Merely hearing an aircraft call meant that it was quite close to the listening station. Telling the aircraft where the listening station was located, therefore, might well give the crew information enough to re-start their own navigation. Conversely, the aircraft could be directed towards the nearest airfield, each telephone-alerted listening station en route refining the direction to fly.

Dorsal (turret): a turret mounted on the top – the back – of the aircraft

Forced-landing/precautionary landing: a forced-landing is a set-down caused by a malfunction which gives the pilot no option but to alight. A precautionary landing is one where the pilot decides that it is politic to put down, so permitting the choice of a suitable site.

'g': acceleration due to gravity. Any high acceleration manoeuvre – change of direction, effectively – results in a change of weight, or of centrifugal force, which is categorised as measuring so many 'g'.

Geodetic: the structure developed by aircraft designer Sir Barnes Wallis and employed in the Wellington bomber. Essentially, it comprised triangular grids made up of aluminium strips to form a mutually-supporting shell of great strength. More properly, the component parts formed 'geodetic' curves (parts of a circle) on the structure, each element taking the shortest line across the curved surface.

GPS: global positioning system. The satellite navigation system is essentially an American military facility which was opened to civilians in 1983 after an airliner was shot down on straying into a prohibited area. In 2000 accuracy for civilian usage was markedly improved. Like a map and compass, however, a GPS repays study, after which it can be of inestimable value on the moor.

Mach number: named after the Austrian physicist Ernst Mach (1838–1916), this refers to the speed of an aircraft in relation to the speed of sound. So, an aircraft moving at twice the speed of sound travels at Mach 2, one at just 0.95 of sonic speed, Mach 0.95.

Ministry of Defence: created in 1971. Formerly its responsibilities in the matter of crash sites lay with the Air Ministry and the Ministry of Aircraft Production (later, Supply). The existence of the Protection of Military Remains Act 1986, order 2008, has to be acknowledged, but although this forbids unauthorised tampering with crash-sites it says nothing of any higher responsibility, by MOD, to the countryside.

Mission (terminology): throughout the era embracing the Second World War, offensive flights against the enemy were termed missions by the United States Army Air Force and operational sorties – or Ops –, by their RAF counterparts. The standard operational tour required from RAF crews may be taken as thirty.

Occult: an aerodrome beacon, alternatively known as an aerial lighthouse, whose white beam was periodically-shaded (that is, occluded) to show a single identifying letter in morse. The beam of this 'occulting searchlight' could be re-directed to point towards an active airfield and was designed to be visible for 'up to thirty miles'.

Posthumous award: American decorations could all be awarded after death. Of British decorations only the Victoria Cross and the George Cross (and the Mention in Despatches) could so bestowed, until 1979.

Power response: on a piston engine, opening the throttle produces an immediate power response. On a jet engine, however, there is a lag while the power response builds up. Using power with flaps ('power against brake': anathema in the piston era), therefore, means more power is already being demanded, hence a more rapid response.

Pundit: an airfield identification beacon, designed to be visible at a range 'not exceeding fifteen miles in good weather', which flashed a two-letter identifier in morse.

Ranger patrols: very long-ranging offensive patrols, flown by Mosquitoes in particular, which sought out enemy aircraft, in the air and on the ground, throughout occupied Europe and the Baltic.

Satellite airfield: an airfield offering flying facilities but administered from a nearby station.

Simple Altimeter: a late-1930's pressure altimeter calibrated according to the Isothermal Law. This assumed a constant temperature of 10°C at all altitudes and a constant sea-level pressure of 1013.2 millibars. During the war the Simple Altimeter was superseded by altimeters calibrated to a more sophisticated International Standard Atmosphere.

Special Operations Executive (SOE): a organisation of volunteers set up in July 1940 to carry out sabotage and subversion behind enemy lines. Churchill described its purpose as being to 'set Europe ablaze'.

Standard Beam Approach (SBA): in essence, this was a radar landing aid which transmitted a 30 mile long, very narrow radio beam down the extended centre-line of the runway. This told a pilot receiving the aural 'on-the-beam' signal that he was somewhere along the projected centre-line of the runway. To furnish an exact location *along* the beam, an 'Outer Marker' radio beacon was sited at a known distance from touchdown. This sent a coded signal vertically upwards to tell an inbound pilot that he should commence his final approach, descending at a rate of 600 feet a minute. There was also a mirror-image back beam, which could be used for landing when the surface wind dictated, although it had no range marker.

Stick (control column): certainly, from the fifties this was always the preferred term among pilots; 'pole' was equally acceptable but somewhat informal, 'joystick' almost antediluvially archaic, and 'control column' too pedantic even for Central Flying School. So stick it is, even where the aircraft in question had a wheel, or a yoke.

Very pistol, sometimes **Very's pistol** (In this book, p137, verey): a breach-loading, wide-bored signalling handgun firing cartridge flares of various colours, named for its 1877 inventor, American naval officer Edward Wilson Very. The reference in this book is misapplied, a layman describing a wingtip landing flare as a Very.

Virtuti Militari: the senior Polish decoration for gallantry. Though it has five classes, with most aircrew receiving the fifth grade, it may be loosely regarded as a Victoria Cross equivalent (pronounced, ver-tooty meellee-tar-eee).

White Instrument Rating: under the contemporary RAF system for showing competence in instrument flying, the White rating was the workaday standard. However, many day-fighter fighter pilots, and even Central Flying School qualified flying instructors, only held White cards, their short sortie lengths (but certainly not their competence) preventing them from gaining the hours necessary for holding the Green, or Master Green held by most Coastal and Transport pilots. The civilian standard is set by the Instrument Rating. As my CFS instructor, a former fighter-jock, and lacking the qualifying hours for anything but a white-card, observed, 'If I had a Master Green like you do, Pat, and flew like that, I'd be ----ing ashamed of myself'.

Wreck: a misnomer employed by air-crash enthusiasts seeking an elegant variation on 'air crash'. Any class of air-craft may be wrecked if it is on the ground but the nautical model, though legitimately transferred in the railway context, is misemployed for machines which come to grief in flight. Notwithstanding this, mainstream aviation usage accepts wreckage, as a synonym for debris.

2. Walking

Abeam: lying at right angles to the line of march. All things being equal, if an established path is followed until a site is directly off one's shoulder, then the least amount of rough walking is required to reach that site.

Col: a depression or lowered section on a hill range.

Clough: a water-carved ravine leading from an upland peat moor. Most Peakland cloughs leave the rim in a steep river of boulders which look daunting but offer many routes through. Any too-steep pitches can be circumvented by backtracking a few yards.

Convex: used of a slope. From the rim the slope bellies outwards, so preventing a view of the ground immediately below.

Degrees magnetic: measuring a track on the map will give the true direction. Adding (pragmatically) five degrees will give the direction to set on the compass. So, a measured track of 070° is set on the compass ring as 075°. (Purists – and enthusiasts – will blanch, but the rest of us will be tramping heather for no more than half a mile or so.)

Grough: a water-carved gully in an upland peat moor, often 20 feet deep. The peat is soot-black, and just as greasy. Egress, however, is always to be found within a few yards. Groughs, when going in the right direction, can afford easy passage.

Hag: the basically firm heather or bilberry stretches of ground left by the deep-cutting groughs.

Yards/Metres: again, let purists go pale, but to the workaday walker these are interchangeable up to half a mile or so.

ACKNOWLEDGEMENTS

To the pioneering, joint authors of the two *Dark Peak Aircraft Wreck* books (1979 and 1982) who paved the way for all walkers puzzled by metal fragments chanced upon while traversing the Peakland Moors. To Ron Collier 1935–2011: Phil Shaw, a field companion, remembers how Ron tramped the moors in the seventies 'with nothing but a compass, hearsay, and myths to go on, so that locating a wreck often took him weeks'; additionally Ron devoted 25 years to the Air Training Corps and qualified as a private pilot. To Roni Wilkinson, who, as an author of boys' stories, set the tone for Ron's findings, serialising the material in the *Barnsley Chronicle* and subsequently joining Pen & Sword Books Ltd.

To veteran air-crash researchers John Ownsworth and Alan Jones (a noted aviation artist), both of whom furnished much extra-archival detail. This also applies to David W. Earl, author of the *Hell on High Ground* books.

To Malcolm Barrass, whose superlative website *Air of Authority* (www.rafweb.org) is a never-failing and utterly dependable source.

To Paul Dalling, for editing the manuscript, and to Simon Hartshorne for creating the book.

To Clive Teale, aviator and grammarian, for technical advice. Similarly to Ken Johnson and Ken Clare for down-to-earth criticism.

To Professor Sean Moran, of Wirksworth, who supplied 'links' enabling the quality of enthusiast web-forum observations to be assessed and who subsequently became a companion on many treks.

To the several hundred folk interviewed, particularly from busy farming families, who gave their time to the research for this series.

To the ever-ebullient – and consistently irreverent – personnel of the Four Seasons Café, Park Farm, Derby; The Wheatcroft's Wharf Café, Cromford; Caudwell's Mill Café, Rowsley; ASDA/Macdonald's, Spondon; Croots Farm Shop, Duffield; and in particular, Hobb's Tea Rooms, Monsal Head.

To the National Trust staff at Kedleston Hall for both irreverence and forbearance.

To the immeasurable expedition afforded by Google.

To Derwent Living, December 2010 (the coldest in 100 years) during research for this book: for no central heating, and memorable proof-reading in fingerless gloves. More to Derby City Housing Standards who forced them to take action.

To the the oncologists of Derby Royal and Nottingham City Hospitals who, early in 2014, advised me against waiting for mainstream publishers to put this book on their list, and not to start another long one, whether as author, or reader ...

To the RAF Museum, the Imperial War Museum, and to the British Library, for assistance with transcribing wartime map references to modern coordinates.

To the traced copyright holders authorising the use of their photographs: Richard Haigh, manager, intellectual properties, Rolls Royce; Nicola Hunt, intellectual property rights copyright unit, MOD; archives staff, Imperial War Museum; Judy Nokes, licensing adviser, HMSO (Crown Copyright/ MOD); John Ownsworth, for photographs used by Ron Collier; Archives staff, Royal Air Force Museum; Mike Stowe, American crash reports; Julian Temple, archivist, Vickers' Brooklands Museum, Weybridge; and Toni Wilkinson, Pen & Sword Publishing. Craving the indulgence of those for whom all contact attempts have failed.

Despite such inestimable assistance, any errors remaining, and all opinions expressed, are my own.

Pat Cunningham DFM

SELECTIVE REFERENCES

Air Ministry (1941) *Air Navigation Volume 1, AP1234.* London: HMSO

Air Ministry (1943) *Elementary Flying Training, AP1979A.* London: HMSO

Air Ministry (1954) *Flying, Volumes 1 and 2, AP129.* (Sixth edition). London: HMSO

Air Ministry (1960) *Flying Instructor's Handbook,* AP3225D. London: HMSO

Air Ministry (1960) *Pilot's Notes Vampire T.11.* London: HMSO

Barrass, Malcolm (2005) *Air of Authority* (www.rafweb.org), (RAF organisation)

Collier, Ron; Wilkinson, Roni. (1979 1982) *Dark Peak Aircraft Wrecks 1 & 2.* Barnsley: Pen & Sword

Cunningham, Pat (Peakland Air Crashes Series: *The South* (2005); *The Central Area* (2006); *The North* (2006). Ashbourne: Landmark Publishing

Handley Page Ltd (1949) *Forty Years On.* London: Handley Page

Office of Public Sector Information (OPSI) 2008. *Protection of Military Remains Act 1986, order 2008.* London

Smith, Peter J.C. (1988) *Flying Bombs over the Pennines.* Manchester: Neil Richardson

Sturtivant, Ray; Page, Gordon. (1999) '*Air Britain Listings*' series. Old Woking: Unwin

Thetford, Owen (1958) *Aircraft of the Royal Air Force 1918-58.* London: Putnam

ND - #0191 - 270225 - C0 - 234/156/14 - PB - 9781780913742 - Gloss Lamination